RELIGIONS IN JAPAN

Religions in Japan

Buddhism, Shinto, Christianity

from the report prepared by the Religions and Cultural
Resources Division, Civil Information and Education
Section, General Headquarters of the Supreme Commander for the Allied Powers, Tokyo, March 1948,
under the editorial direction of

William K. Bunce

CHARLES E. TUTTLE COMPANY
RUTLAND, VERMONT   TOKYO, JAPAN

*Published by the Charles E. Tuttle
Company of Rutland, Vermont and
Tokyo, Japan, with editorial offices
at 15 Edogawa-cho, Bunkyo-ku, Tokyo,
Japan.*

First Edition, January 1955

*Manufactured in Japan by
Hosokawa Printing Co., Ltd.*

FOREWORD

Publication of this book will meet a long-felt need for an up-to-date, reliable account of a subject of perennial interest. Students of Japanese culture will find here, in readable, non-technical language, answers to their many questions on the complicated and sometimes confusing scene of Japanese religions. Even the scholar may find in these pages new items to arrest his attention or new points of view which may stimulate a reexamination of hitherto accepted interpretations. For the general reader, there exists no better introduction to the vast subject of Japanese religions.

Religions in Japan was a report prepared in 1948 by Civilian Information and Education Section, General Headquarters, Supreme Commander for the Allied Powers. It was originally conceived by officers of the Religions Division as a means of enabling Military Government Teams better to understand problems encountered in the field of religion—as a handbook which would give historical perspective and provide concise and reliable information and an understanding of the significance of Occupation Policy as it related to religion.

The work of research for the volume and preparation of the manuscript was shared jointly by the Religions Division of CI & E and the Religions Research Branch of Analysis and Research Division of CI & E. As officer in charge of the Religions

Research Branch, it was my duty to supervise the research and preparation of the drafts on the chapters describing the various religions and sects of Japan. We were fortunate in having on our staff a group of Japanese advisors—Buddhist, Shinto, and Christian priests, ministers, and scholars—who were ideally qualified to carry out the assignment, and to them and to my associate, Miss Takako Yamada, must go the credit for the accuracy and objectivity of the report. The Religions Division was responsible for the planning, editing, and final preparation of the book and for the manuscripts for the first chapter, giving a brief history of religions in Japan, and for the chapter on Occupation policy. Dr. W. K. Bunce, currently Acting Chief Public Affairs Officer of the United States Embassy in Tokyo, was chief of Religions Division, and his assistants were Mr. George A. Warp, now professor of Political Science at the University of Minnesota and Mr. Walter Nichols, who is currently Field Supervisor of the United States Information Service in Tokyo.

As soon as the book was published by General Headquarters, it was distributed to key offices in the Occupation and to selected educational institutions in the United States. The response was highly favorable, and demand greatly exceeded the supply. Thus, this present publication should be a welcome development for those who have been trying unsuccessfully all these years to get their hands on one of the original copies.

The publishers of the present edition of the book have deleted much of the material in the last chapter of the original publication, which was of interest only to persons directly concerned with implementing the programs of the Occupation or was only of topical interest when the book was written. However, all material of lasting and contemporary significance has been left intact, and the resulting publication is one which should prove of interest and value to anyone looking for a good introduction to the fascinating subject of Japanese religions.

A few comments on developments in Japanese religions since the book was written may be in order. The establishment of religious freedom was experienced as a distinct shock by the religious world of Japan. Then gradually there came a glimmer of what freedom meant or what it could mean. Many Buddhist temples and Shinto shrines are still floundering in bewilderment, not knowing how to adjust themselves to the current situation. Yet there seems to be evidence that the old sense of dependence on the government is weakening. A progressive new leadership has gradually begun to assert itself. Shinto shrines have definitely started on a new path. One department of the Shrine Association is engaged in developing shrine doctrine and training of priests to preach! Many laymen are taking a new interest in their shrines and seem to be anxious to participate in them on a democratic basis. Inevitably, the establishment of religious freedom releases great stores of social energy. Whether shrines and temples can and will adjust themselves permanently to the ways of a free society or will move in the direction of the revival of the authoritarian system, I cannot prophesy. But as the situation stands today, it will be *their* choice, and there are many who wish to move forward in accordance with their new freedom.

The present trend of Japanese Buddhism seems to be in the direction of closer ties and greater cooperation with Buddhists of other countries, with the purpose of unity in world Buddhism and the establishment of world peace.

Christianity continues to grow, but the rate of increase has slowed down somewhat. The International Christian University now has a strong faculty and has admitted its second class. The National Christian Council has been reorganized with four denominations and several non-denominational organizations, representing more than 80% of the Protestant community.

FOREWORD

Among the thirteen sects of Sectarian Shinto, Tenri-kyo continues to show the greatest vigor. Its financial strength appears to be phenomenal. Konko-kyo, although troubled by internal disputes, is likewise vigorous. Its largest "church," the Izuo Kyokai in Osaka, claims 100,000 members, who are affiliated with some twenty subordinate churches scattered throughout the country. Taisha-kyo merged some years ago with the Grand Shrine of Izumo and withdrew from the Sectarian Shinto Federation. The status of the other nine sects is not clear. It would appear that, with Shinto shrines now engaging in vigorous activity, the future of some of the sects is rather precarious.

While there is some agitation against the so-called new religions, the stronger ones have gone steadily ahead both in numerical strength and institutional effectiveness. The third anniversary of the founding of the Union of New Religious Organizations of Japan, which is composed of more than fifty constituent bodies, has just been observed.

Perhaps the greatest danger to religious freedom lies in the desire of many leaders of the established religions for more control of the so-called "new religions." It is impossible to predict to what extent they will go in urging this control, but it hard to escape the feeling that much of the agitation is an expression of the urge for self-preservation, rather than genuine moral indignation over alleged violations of laws or accepted customs. How easy it for some to forget the time when their own faith was suspect because it was new!

Tokyo, Japan
November 15, 1954

WILLIAM P. WOODARD
Director of the International Institute
for the Study of Religions in Japan

CONTENTS

FOREWORD v

1. DEVELOPMENT OF JAPANESE RELIGIONS 1
   Primitive Religion and Legends 1
   Introduction of Buddhism and the Nara Period 4
   Heian Period and Ryobu Shinto 8
   Kamakura Period and the Great Spiritual Awakening . . 12
   Ashikaga Period and the "Dark Ages" 17
   Unification of Japan and the Introduction of Christianity . 20
   Tokugawa Period and the Meiji Restoration 23

2. ROLE OF GOVERNMENT IN RELIGIOUS LIFE 27
   Attempts to Establish a Theocratic State 27
   Creation and Development of the Shrine Board 30
   Control of Religion 33
   Religious Organizations and the Government 34
   Militarism in Religion, 1931–1941 37
   Militarism in Religion, 1941–1945 39
   Postwar Adjustments 42

3. BUDDHISM: ORIGIN AND NATURE 44

4. BUDDHISM: INSTITUTIONAL ASPECTS 49
   Sect Organization 49
   The Priesthood 51
   Temples 53
   Scriptures, Sacred Utensils, and Services 55

ix

CONTENTS

5. BUDDHISM: DESCRIPTION OF SECTS 58
   The Nara Sects 59
   Tendai Buddhism 61
   Shingon Buddhism 69
   Amida Buddhism 74
   Zen Buddhism 87
   Nichiren Buddhism 92

6. SHINTO: NATURE AND TYPES 98
   Primitive Shinto 99
   Early Mythology 102
   Foreign Influences 104
   Types of Shinto 106
   Tennoism 108
   Imperial Family Shinto 110
   Popular Beliefs 112

7. SHINTO: SHRINE 115
   The Priesthood 118
   Shrine Buildings 119
   Worship 120
   Types of Shrines 121

8. SHINTO: SECTARIAN 129
   Pure Shinto Sects 132
   Confucian Sects 135
   Mountain Sects 136
   Purification Sects 139
   Sects of Peasant Origin 141

9. CHRISTIANITY 148
   Early Christianity in Japan 148
   Christianity in Modern Japan 151
   Christian Welfare Work 155
   Christian Education 157

CONTENTS

10. NEW SECTS 160
    Monotheistic Group 162
    Henotheistic Group 163
    Shinto Polytheistic Group 163
    Messianic Group 164
    Group Subject to Chinese Influence 165

11. IMPACT OF OCCUPATION ON JAPANESE RELIGIONS 166

APPENDIX: STATISTICS OF RELIGIOUS SECTS AND DENOMINATIONS . 173

GLOSSARY OF RELIGIOUS TERMS 181

BIBLIOGRAPHY 187

INDEX 191

RELIGIONS IN JAPAN

1

DEVELOPMENT OF JAPANESE RELIGIONS

Primitive Religion and Legends

Little is known of the early Japanese, and much that is written about Japanese history prior to the Christian era is pure speculation based on archaeological discoveries, racial characteristics, and legends. Historians agree, however, that, in about the first century of the Christian era, there was a Mongoloid invasion of southern and central Japan via Korea. These invaders organized themselves into small clans and, in the course of a few centuries, the Yamato clan, which took its name from the plain in which it finally settled, established a vague suzerainty over the whole of central and southern Japan.

The religion of these early Japanese was a polytheistic nature worship. They believed that all natural phenomena were of animistic character and that each person or thing was in itself a manifestation of the divine. Though all things were thought individually to possess a spirit, there was no conception of an immortal soul and no philosophical speculation on life and death. The anthropomorphic concept of deities no doubt existed, as evidenced by legends and myths about the creation of the universe, but the deities of the primitive Japanese pantheon were not well defined, and their powers and characters were very nebulous.

1

Anything which evoked a feeling of awe was revered as being particularly imbued with divine or mysterious power; therefore, the forces of nature, especially awe-inspiring trees, rocks, or mountains, and other inexplicable natural phenomena became objects of worship. These were given the name *kami*.

Before any system of government existed, there were festivals and religious rites. Persons thought to possess occult power or spiritual insight, many of whom were women, acted as priests and performed religious rites in which they called forth divine power by means of sorcery, divination, and lustration. These ceremonies were usually purification rites to guard against pollution and decay, or thanksgiving for harvests and the favors of nature. As the necessity for clan solidarity gave rise to the recognition of hereditary rights and authority, the clan chieftain took over the function of high priest. It was to his interest that social stability prevail, and he saw to it that the tutelary deities or spirits upon whose favor the welfare of his people depended were properly respected. Apparently, there was very little distinction between his administrative and priestly functions. The clan chieftain, acting as high priest, eventually came to be regarded as a superior being. He was himself referred to as a *kami* and was revered after his death. This corollary of nature worship, so common among primitive peoples and religions, was undoubtedly an early form of ancestor worship, but it remained for the later introduction of Confucianism to spread the cult of ancestor worship through all classes of Japanese society.

As the conquering Yamato clan spread its authority over the country, its legends and deities gained pre-eminence over those of the lesser clans, and its chieftain began to perform certain special rites on behalf of all of the people. In this manner, the chiefs of the Yamato clan in the third or fourth century became not only the actual rulers of a loosely organized state, but also the chief priests of the nation, and it is from these priest-chiefs that the present imperial family claims descent.

The legends of the Yamato clan became in time the basis for popular belief in the divine origin and superiority of the Japanese race. The Yamato brought with them from the continent a form of sun worship, and the fountainhead of their legends was a cosmogonic myth. The early mythology of the Japanese began with an account of two deities, Izanagi and Izanami, who descended from "the high plain of heaven" and created the islands of Japan, with all their mountains, rivers, grasses, and trees, and of the Sun Goddess, Amaterasu Omikami, and a multitude of lesser deities. Amaterasu Omikami eventually sent her grandson, Ninigi-no-mikoto, to rule over Japan, and his great-grandson, Jimmu Tenno, became the first Yamato ruler. The traditional regalia of the Yamato rulers were a mirror, a jewel, and a sword, probably representing the sun, the moon, and the lightning, and these were regarded as symbols of authority given by the Sun Goddess to Ninigi-no-mikoto. With the ascendancy of the Yamato clan, this solar myth was accepted by the other clans and became the popular theory concerning the origin of the Japanese race, while the mirror, jewel, and sword became the emblems of imperial authority.

Between the third and sixth centuries, Japan was subjected to various continental influences through contact with Korea. In the year 405, a Korean scholar named Wani introduced Confucian practical ethics. Some aspects of Taoist dualism were also imported. But neither was brought in as an organized religion, their influence taking the form of a subtle penetration of social customs and legends. Contact with Korea and China in minor warlike expeditions brought the Japanese in touch with Buddhism also, but there appears to have been no Buddhist activity of any consequence in Japan prior to the sixth century.

Introduction of Buddhism and the Nara Period

Buddhism was officially introduced in 552 when the hard-pressed monarch of a small kingdom on the Korean peninsula sent an embassy to Japan seeking military assistance. His emissaries carried presents, including a small image of Buddha and several sutras, or scriptures. In a letter, the king recommended Buddhism as an efficacious religion, promising that it would bring happiness and good fortune. The Yamato sovereign officially permitted the head of a prominent court family to try out the new religion. It should be noted that this was done partly for political reasons since Japan, which by this time had been organized into a fairly consolidated nation, wished to form an alliance with Korean kingdoms. In the meantime, there was an influx of Buddhist missionaries and scholars from Korea and China, who brought with them evidence of a vastly superior continental civilization. There was strong opposition to Buddhism on the part of conservative leaders and the superstitious masses of the people. These feared that disloyalty to the native gods would cause divine retribution. A growing number of liberal-minded Japanese, however, were attracted to the new religion by its superiority over the native cults. A long period of conflict ensued which culminated in a complete victory for the liberal, pro-Buddhist forces in 593. A female sovereign, Suiko, was placed on the throne, and Shotoku Taishi, a devout Buddhist scholar, assumed control of the government as prince-regent.

After Shotoku became regent, it was not long before Buddhism dominated the religious life of the court. In 604, it became in effect the state religion, its function being to secure divine support for official policies. The second article of the moral injunctions issued by Shotoku reads in part: "Revere sincerely the three treasures—Buddha, the law, and the church

4

—for these are . . . the supreme object of faith in all countries."
During the Asuka period (592–628) the heads of many great
families adopted Buddhism and vied with each other in building
magnificent Buddhist temples. A great number of Japanese
scholars and religious leaders were sent to China for study and
training, and some later traveled as far as India. In the intercourse which developed with China and Korea, Buddhism became
the main channel of continental influence.

With the introduction of Chinese civilization on a large
scale, Japan emerged from the primitive stage of her existence.
The significance for later Japanese history of the wholesale importation through Buddhism of philosophy, logic, art, the rudi-
ments of psychology and natural science, and the more highly
developed agricultural and engineering techniques can hardly
be overestimated. The influence of Buddhism on the spiritual
and cultural life of the court during the Nara period (628–784)
was tremendous. Its impact on the administration of the government was equally great. Confucian ethics and the practical
politics embodied in its teachings revolutionized the Japanese
concept of the state. As communications with the continent im-
proved, the Japanese were deeply impressed by the might and
grandeur of the Chinese government, and they earnestly set about
to develop a similar system. This effort culminated in the great
Taika Reform of 646 which gave Japan a government modeled
on that of the Confucian-based government of China. Progressive
leaders, aware that the old clan deities could not meet the needs
of a more consolidated national community, regarded Buddhism
as a powerful aid in promoting national prosperity. Government
support of the new religion was so far-reaching that, in 655, an
official decree was issued ordering the construction of *butsudan*,
small Buddhist altars, in all households of the nation.

It must not be supposed, however, that the native religion

died out. Early Buddhism in Japan employed Chinese architecture, costumes, rites, and language and made little effort to adapt itself to Japanese life. For this reason, it did not quickly penetrate the life of the people in general. It became the religion of the elite, who had the education necessary to appreciate in some measure its difficult philosophies. For the masses, the primitive religion had to suffice. Moreover, despite the great favor shown to Buddhism by the court, there was a significant revival of the native religion towards the end of the seventh century. It was now given the name *Shinto* (way of the gods) to distinguish it from *Buppo* (way of the Buddha). Shinto had by this time developed a dual nature: it retained the simple, animistic ritualism of the traditional nature worship, and it produced an elaborate cult deliberately fostered by the Yamato clan as a political expedient. The Sun Goddess was the central figure of this cult. Belief in the divine origin through her of the ruling family was employed for the consolidation of political power. By the sixth century, the Sun Goddess cult had been accepted by the whole nation, the Sun Goddess shrine at Ise was a national sanctuary, and ceremonies were conducted there by virgin imperial princesses. As a result of the Taika Reform, a Department of Shrines (*Jingikan*) under the administration of an imperial prince was established independent of the Cabinet. This department was given charge of rites and festivals stipulated in national laws, and Shinto began more and more to assume the aspects of an official cult.

Shinto had been very nearly overwhelmed in official circles by the introduction of Buddhism, but, as previously stated, the new religion was slow in penetrating to the masses of the people. When the Japanese began to conceive of their nation as an empire and set about to rival the glory and might of China, the Sun Goddess cult proved a convenient vehicle for the glorification of the nation and its ruler. While exerting every effort to import from China the practical benefits of a superior civilization, the Japanese attempted to enhance their race through assertion of divine origin. It is noteworthy that about this time the Japanese first began to speak of their ruler as an emperor.

The *Nihongi* and the *Kojiki*, official chronicles of the times, devoted much space to early mythology and the "age of the gods." They have played a remarkably important role in Japanese history, because they were resurrected in the nineteenth century by super-patriots as the basis for the restoration of imperial rule and were later used as arguments for belief in the divine mission of Japan and the sovereignty of its emperor over all the peoples of the earth. It is difficult to determine how much of the *Nihongi* was based on actual native mythology and how much of it was invented to glorify the imperial family, but it evidences foreign influence in parts and, as an official chronicle, contains many historical absurdities. It served its purpose, however, and became the bible of Shinto. Thus, during the seventh and eighth centuries, while the religious and intellectual life of the court was dominated by Buddhist and Confucian thought, Shinto remained the religion of the people and also became almost a part of the political machinery.

Under the patronage of the imperial court, Buddhism prospered. The early missionaries and scholars wisely refrained from making sectarian distinctions, realizing that the Japanese were not intellectually mature enough to appreciate the finer points of doctrinal variations. But, after a period of about 70 years, sectarian differences appeared in Japan, and eventually six sects were introduced from China. These were the Sanron (625), Jojitsu (625), Hosso (654), Kusha (658), Kegon (736), and Ritsu (754) sects. In the Asuka period, Buddhism had gained a hold on the upper classes, and, in the Nara period, it extended its influence into the field of politics. Although the imperial succession is claimed to be "unbroken for ages eternal," the Asuka and Nara periods witnessed frequent succession quarrels, abdications, assassinations, and struggles within the major families of the ruling clan. In the confusion of the times, Buddhist monks grew increasingly powerful in the capital at Nara. The court lavished expenditures on temples and priests, Buddhism became an increasingly aristocratic religion, and a presumptuous and corrupt hierarchy emerged within the monasteries. It was not uncommon for emperors, tired of the political wrangling and the rigidity of court rituals, to abdicate and seek political immunity in Buddhist orders. Under such circumstances, it is not surprising that the monasteries grew enormously wealthy and acquired vast, tax-free estates. Ambitious priests became involved in political intrigues; one grasping prelate, Dokyo, even attempted unsuccessfully to have himself made imperial consort.

But the very power of Nara Buddhism proved its downfall. The sects were literary and scholastic and lacked the vitality essential for securing an extensive following outside the ruling classes. The ideological conflict with Shinto, the national cult, presented many difficulties, and the meddling of Buddhist priests in politics became distasteful to certain powerful factions at court. When the Fujiwara family finally won full control over the government, it lost no time in establishing a new capital in order to remove the seat of government from the priest-ridden political extravagances of Nara.

Heian Period and Ryobu Shinto

The removal of the capital to Kyoto in 794 marked the beginning of the Heian period (794–1185), one of the most

8

brilliant in Japanese history. It was ushered in with political and religious reforms, the former effected by the powerful Fujiwara family, the latter by two remarkable leaders who appeared at the turn of the century.

The two men who brought about the transformation in Buddhism were Saicho and Kukai, known posthumously as Dengyo Daishi and Kobo Daishi respectively. The removal of the capital to Kyoto did not mean that the court no longer favored Buddhism. It was merely tired of the secular activities of the Nara priests. Accordingly, Emperor Kwammu dispatched these two men to China to find and bring back a more spiritual form of Buddhism. On their return, Saicho founded the Tendai sect in 805, and Kukai founded the Shingon sect in 809. The teachings of these two leaders and the sects they established dominated the spiritual and cultural life of Japan for centuries. In spite of the opposition of jealous prelates in Nara, the Tendai institutions founded on Mount Hiei by Saicho and the Shingon monasteries built on Mount Koya by Kukai became great centers of learning which aided the popularization of Buddhism.

Both Saicho and Kukai included in their teachings certain concepts which could be grasped even by uneducated people. In addition, they preached that salvation could be attained by the lowliest of men. Nara Buddhism had been an exclusive and discriminating faith. Now, discrimination in favor of the upper classes was done away with, and salvation was made available to all. This universality of salvation was an important factor in popularizing Buddhism. Another factor was the popular appeal of the esoteric practices of Shingon. Kukai's emphasis on the sacred functions of body, speech, and mind, the complicated ritualistic manipulation of hands and fingers, and the incantation of mystic formulae, as well as the promise through them of worldly profit, appealed to the common people. Yet another factor was the eclecticism of Saicho's Tendai philosophy, which endeavored to harmonize the various teachings and schools of thought.

The most important factor in the rapid spread of Buddhism among the lower classes was the merging of Shinto deities with those of the Buddhist pantheon. An attempt to identify the native gods with Buddhist deities had been made in the Nara period, but it was not until the time of Saicho and Kukai that this effort bore fruit. Saicho preached that Buddhist and Shinto deities were identical and succeeded in part in merging the two religions. It remained for Kukai, however, to provide an explanation comprehensible and acceptable to those who maintained their loyalty to the native gods. He propounded a new incarnation theory which stipulated that the eternal Buddha appears in different forms at various places in order to save mankind. By extension of this theory, he argued that the national deities of Shinto were incarnations of Buddhas and Bodhisattvas and thus, since there was no distinction between the worship of Buddhist deities and those of Shinto, that there were no basically conflicting elements in the two religions. He identified Buddha with the Sun Goddess and lesser Buddhist deities with lesser Shinto deities. This combination of the two religions he called *Ryobu* (dual aspect) Shinto.

Ryobu Shinto was not a merger of the two organizations such as that which usually characterizes the amalgamation of two groups. It was a subtle ideological coalescence of a deeper nature which enabled the two to exist together. As we have seen, Shinto accepted Buddhism by adding to its pantheon the foreign deities from China and India. Buddhism, however, approached the matter from a different angle. It declared that Shinto deities were derivative manifestations of the Buddhist deities which were regarded as original entities. The boundaries in this fusion became more and more obliterated. Buddhist priests took charge of Shinto sanctuaries, and Shinto priests began to play only minor parts in the ceremonies. With the ascendancy of Buddhism, Shinto ceased to occupy a position of prominence. Shrines were largely the property of families who, with the approval of the government, placed members trained for the Buddhist priesthood in charge of them. Worshippers were almost unable to make a distinction between the two religions. Indeed, the Buddhist influence became so strong that the form of Shinto rituals and celebrations, the decorative effects in the shrines, and even the images of the native deities took on a decidedly Buddhist flavor. However, the amalgamation was never complete. There developed a division of duties: Shinto deities presided over the affairs of this world, while the life hereafter became the concern of Buddhism. Births, marriages, seasonal festivals, and victories in battle were in the sphere of Shinto interest. Preaching doctrinal matters, ecclesiastical organization, and funerals were the responsibility of Buddhism. Ancestor worship, however, which under strong Confucian influence had become a universal practice, was the affair of both. Through exorcism and divination, some Shinto shrines entered the field of teaching and doctrine, but Shinto was definitely subordinated to the Buddhist hierarchy.

From the ninth to the twelfth centuries, Japan enjoyed peace and prosperity. During this period, the foreign culture imported during the Asuka and Nara periods was absorbed into a new and distinctive Japanese culture. The Heian period produced great achievements in art, literature, and architecture and clearly showed Japanese inventiveness. The Japanese applied their own creative genius to original Chinese patterns and no longer relied on China for inspiration. But, though the greatest cultural achievements in Japanese history were attained in this period, it was not long before a slow decay began to eat away the foundations of this culture. The government, which had been modeled on the T'ang government of China, grew more and more decentralized as local aristocrats and influential families built up their power and prestige. The court itself became effete and corrupt. Monasteries again became politically and financially powerful. Despite the earnest desires of Saicho and Kukai to promote social welfare, their followers of the tenth and eleventh centuries began to devote themselves mainly to rituals and incantations and to serve the powerful aristocrats whose bountiful gifts they eagerly sought. In time, they became so corrupt that they even maintained virtual armies of monk-soldiers with which to intimidate courtiers through whom they sought influence at the imperial court. Although Buddhism was the dominant religion of the day and had driven Shinto into the background, it failed to exercise any direct or enduring influence on the everyday spiritual life of the people. The early twelfth century was a time of political and religious stagnation, but in 1185, after nearly four centuries of relative ease and peace, there was a revolution in which the decadent Kyoto government was overthrown. The administrative government was removed to Kamakura, leaving in the capital the powerless emperor, his imperial court, and its vast following of effete aristocrats and meddling monks.

Kamakura Period and the Great Spiritual Awakening

The removal of the political center from Kyoto to Kamakura signaled a great change in the trend of Japanese history. The culture of the upper classes had to a considerable degree penetrated to the masses. Plain warriors from common stock had defeated the refined but degenerate court nobles. In the Kamakura period (1185–1333), the predominant influences in the country were expressions of the times and not modifications of

12

foreign importations. The Hojo family set up in Kamakura a strong and efficient feudal government and carried out extensive reforms.

At the beginning of the Heian period, an effort had been made by Saicho and Kukai to spread Buddhism throughout all classes of people. This movement, however, had been only partly successful, because Buddhism was by tradition so centered around court life that the followers of these two leaders soon lost interest in the popularization of their faith and again catered to the needs of the aristocracy. In the process of performing these functions, Buddhism had itself become secularized. The great temples of the period grew financially powerful and drew local or minor temples and large estates into their control. Since the Fujiwara clan could not support its increasing numbers, many entered the priesthood and received the finest sinecures, becoming chief priests in the great head temples. But, along with their priestly duties, they continued to participate in secular affairs.

Degenerate as was the priesthood, there were a few sincere men who were not corrupted by the accessibility of worldly profit. They realized that elaborate doctrinal systems and ostentatious rituals did not meet the needs of the people and felt that a revival of true religion was needed. They attempted a revival of the older Nara sects, which had been in eclipse for some three centuries, but, though this revival was remarkable for its scholarship and monastic discipline, it did not affect the people in large numbers.

Vital religious life for the twelfth century was not to be found in any revival. Something new was required. The confusion in the closing years of the Heian period turned the minds of the people to the hope of better things to come, and their expectation was fulfilled in the great spiritual awakening which marked the end of the Heian and the beginning of the Kamakura periods. Tendai had within it seeds which fructified under the catalyzing influence of dynamic leaders. Unable to endure any longer the conflict in doctrines which Saicho had attempted to harmonize in Tendai, these men founded new sects based on Tendai teachings. The religious movements which they initiated still constitute the dominant Buddhist influences of the country. The teachings of these leaders were reactions against the aristocratic Buddhism of the Heian period. They founded religions for common people. Metaphysical elaborations were set aside and incomprehensible practices were made secondary or of less import. By simple, direct affirmations they gave an answer to the spiritual quest of the common man.

The first significant development in the religious revival was the rapid spread of Amidaism. It had been included in the teachings of Saicho in the ninth century and had materially aided the first popularization of Buddhism, but there was no widespread propagation of Amidaism until the twelfth century. Amida Buddhism had a great popular appeal, because it offered salvation on relatively easy terms. The other schools of Buddhism required spiritual enlightenment for salvation and demanded of their followers rigid discipline and much personal effort, whereas Amidaism demanded of its followers only one thing—absolute faith in the Buddha Amida. Rebirth in the Western Paradise was promised to all those who merely called on the name of Amida in simple faith. This new doctrine of salvation through the power of another quite naturally appealed to the masses, who did not have the leisure to master the difficult practices of the Tendai, Shingon, and Nara sects. The first Amida sect to appear was the Yuzu Nembutsu sect, which was founded as early as 1117, but it contained much of the teachings of the older schools. Amidaism did not come into its own until a Tendai priest named Honen founded the Jodo sect in 1175. Honen was succeeded by an outstanding disciple named Shinran, who founded the Jodo Shin sect in 1224, and the doctrines of these two reformers spread rapidly among the less-educated people.

The second major development in the great spiritual awakening was the introduction of Zen Buddhism. Zen, like Amidaism, was known in Japan in the Nara period, but its teachings did not become the basis for a new school of Buddhism until a Tendai priest named Eisai founded the Rinzai sect in 1191. The Soto sect, founded by Dogen in 1244, helped to spread Zen philosophy. By the fourteenth century, Zen Buddhism had become the most influential religion in Japan. Essentially, Zen was more a philosophy than a religion. Its adherents engaged in silent meditation and abstract contemplation and attempted through mental discipline to attain an intuitive perception of the fundamental truth of reality. Zen required of its followers complete detachment of the self from all transitory phenomena and from concern for personal gain. Its strict spiritual discipline secured for it many followers among the warrior class, who found that Zen gave them courage in battle and self-reliance in administration.

The third and last significant movement in this remarkable period of Japan's religious history was the appearance of a fiery reformer named Nichiren. He believed that all the sectarian interpretations of his day, including Amidaism and Zen, were perversions of Buddhism's true meaning. After studying at the Tendai institution on Mount Hiei, he eventually decided that true Buddhism was to be found only in the teachings of the Lotus Sutra, and he therefore set about to reform Japanese Buddhism. He began to preach the doctrines of the Lotus Sutra and proclaimed that anyone who recited the sacred formula "Adoration to the sutra of the lotus of the true law" would receive moral virtue and attain paradise on this earth. But he also began to denounce the teachings of the established sects as heresies and even attacked the policies of the government in Kamakura. Though he was persecuted mercilessly by both ecclesiastical and political authorities, his supporters soon numbered many thousands and were so imbued with the indomitable spirit of Nichiren that they became a vital factor in the religious life of the nation. It was in the year 1253 that Nichiren first proclaimed his doctrine of the Lotus Sutra, and his followers, who later formed the Nichiren sect, date the origin of their faith from that occasion.

During the course of the centuries, Buddhism had been regarded by many as a foreign religion, thus retarding its assimilation into the national life. But, with the great spiritual awakening of the Kamakura period, Buddhism became truly indigenous. Shingon, Tendai, and some of the Nara sects continued to maintain their following, but three of the earliest sects—Sanron, Jojitsu, and Kusha—did not survive the rising tide of Amidaism, Zen, and Nichirenism which swept the country. It is interesting to note that the seeds of each of these new doctrines had been present in the eclectic Tendai philosophy expounded by Saicho in the ninth century. The monasteries he founded on Mount Hiei may be called the fountainhead of the religious revival, since Honen, Shinran, Eisai, Dogen, Nichiren, and the other religious leaders of the twelfth and thirteenth centuries first studied there and selected from Tendai doctrines the particular philosophies which became the foundation of their faiths.

Although the new sects of the Kamakura period became in time the most powerful forces in the religious world of Japan, they did not achieve their ascendancy without bitter opposition. The rapid spread of the new doctrines aroused jealousy and enmity among the clergy of the established sects. Often on the most trivial grounds they attempted to suppress these rival faiths. The Tendai priests of Mount Hiei frequently resorted to force. Honen, the great founder of the Amida school, was so feared by his jealous rivals that even the emperor was persuaded to take sides in the issue. Honen was banished from the capital in 1207. In the same year, his disciple Shinran was also banished. Their exile, however, only lent opportunity to their activities since it freed them to engage in active evangelism among the people of outlying areas. Zen Buddhism, with its emphasis on rigid spiritual discipline and intuitive perception, was not readily welcomed by the priests of the older sects or even by the priests of the new Amida and Nichiren sects. Nichiren was so persecuted for his bitter attacks on the alleged intellectual degeneracy of all the sects of his day and for his political judgments that he not only was hounded from place to place by his ecclesiastical opponents but was twice exiled by the Kamakura government. Once he was sentenced to death for heresy and inciting rebellion, although this sentence was commuted to exile. In the fourteenth and fifteenth centuries, the soldier-monks of Mount Hiei again and again descended from their stronghold to attack and burn to the ground the head temples of the Amida and Nichiren sects. In 1344, they held mass meetings of protest and criticized the court for tolerating Zen priests, whom they called demons and enemies of the state. But nothing could stop the rapid growth of the new sects, which received so much support in spite of the persecutions that they eventually became the most important schools of Buddhism.

Ashikaga Period and the "Dark Ages"

The Kamakura period lasted only a century and a half. The clique of warrior families which had seized power in 1185 gradually dissolved. Two Mongol invasions in 1274 and 1281 were successfully repulsed, but they served to weaken the central authority and to scatter the military forces of the Kamakura rulers. Famine and disease plagued the nation. The government finally became so disorganized that an abortive attempt was made to restore imperial rule. In 1333, a Kamakura general named Ashikaga Takauji was ordered to subdue this rebellion, but he marched on Kamakura instead, destroyed the government there, and in 1338, set himself up in Kyoto as shogun. There he attempted to create a central government. The Ashikaga shoguns who succeeded him managed to retain a loose control over the country for 200 years, but there was never any effective rule during the Ashikaga period (1333-1568). The warrior class slowly lost its prestige and was replaced by powerful feudal lords who maintained large armies of loyal retainers and did much as they pleased within their own domains. By 1400, these feudal lords, or daimyo, had become so independent that a series of civil wars ensued. Anarchy prevailed towards the end of the fourteenth century, and, by 1500, the whole of Japan was divided into warring factions. It was not until the end of the sixteenth century that Japan again became a united nation.

Although the opening of the Kamakura period witnessed an amazing revival of religious interest among all classes of people, the religious history of the Nara and Heian periods soon began to be repeated. Buddhism, which had become a powerful influence on the spiritual life of the people, again became secularized in the Ashikaga period. The religious enthusiasm which had spread Buddhism to nearly every home in the nation dwindled to almost nothing. Many minor sects appeared within the large sects, few men of stature appeared to carry on the work of the great reformers, and priests and institutions once more became involved in politics. The religious zeal of the reformation disappeared in a general lack of inspiration.

Despite its loss of religious vitality, however, Buddhism dominated the political and cultural life of the nation as never before. Because of the general anarchy prevailing in Japan in this period, historians sometimes refer to the Ashikaga period as the "dark ages." In these turbulent times, the native Shinto religion was almost completely forgotten. The Tendai priests on Mount Hiei continued their violent persecution of the newer sects and intimidated the helpless court. There were incessant minor wars between various factions associated with large temples. Armed monks roamed the streets of the capital, terrorized the populace, and fought duels. Sometimes pitched battles were waged with members of rival institutions. The cause of these altercations were more often political than religious.

Zen Buddhism, owing to its support from the warrior class, became virtually the state religion in the Ashikaga period. In the turmoil of the times, Zen monks performed the same service for culture as the monks of Europe did in the Middle Ages. They were the thinkers and intellectual leaders of their day. In their monasteries, they created and preserved masterpieces of literature and art which otherwise might have been destroyed. They also displayed remarkable practical wisdom; they engaged in business; they perfected new methods of accounting. The most important academies were managed by Zen priests. Ashikaga College, founded in the fourteenth century, became practically the only center of Chinese classical learning. In an age of ambitious prelates and corrupt religion, the Zen priests devoted themselves to education and the betterment of society. They were not beyond embroiling themselves occasionally in intersectarian disputes and political scheming, but they definitely contributed much to Japanese culture while all around them was chaos.

Unification of Japan and the Introduction of Christianity

The unification of Japan was accomplished during what is called the Sengoku period (1568–1615) by three great leaders. Nobunaga, the first of these outstanding figures, became shogun in 1568 and laid the foundations for national unity by fighting campaigns against the rebellious feudatories of western Japan. Upon his death in 1582, he was succeeded by his ablest general, Hideyoshi, who carried on the military campaigns for unification. Hideyoshi very nearly succeeded and became so powerful militarily that he even sent two armies of invasion to subjugate Korea and China. But, upon his death in 1598, the continental campaign was abandoned and the armies withdrawn. Hideyoshi was succeeded by Tokugawa Ieyasu, who proved to be an extraordinarily gifted general and administrator. Ieyasu completed the unification of the nation when, in 1615, he stormed Osaka Castle after having defeated all other opposition and, with all independent elements subjugated, became the first ruler of a united Japan in three centuries. He left the imperial court powerless in Kyoto and set up his military government in Yedo, the present city of Tokyo. The Tokugawa shogunate founded by him maintained its control over Japan for 250 years.

In the first half of the sixteenth century, Japan came in contact with the West for the first time, and, during the unsettled Sengoku period, was subjected to various influences from Europe. In 1542, the Portuguese discovered Japan and, by 1549, St. Francis Xavier, the first Christian missionary to Japan, was spreading the gospel of Christ among the Japanese. He was followed by other Catholic missionaries, whose efforts met with considerable success, especially in Kyushu and the southern parts of the country. Some historians estimate that, by 1600, there were approximately

750,000 Christian converts, but this figure should be treated with caution. It was customary in feudal Japan for loyal retainers to adopt the religion professed by their lords. Since the followers of these men composed the bulk of Japanese Christians, it is open to question how many of them really understood the new religion of their adoption. There even appears to be a strong likelihood that the Japanese first regarded Christianity as a new school of Buddhism. The language barrier and the attendant difficulty which the missionaries encountered in preaching their doctrines no doubt caused much confusion. Since there are many similarities between Buddhism and Christianity, the distinctions could not have been very clear. It is certain that Buddhist leaders did not at first recognize in Christianity a dangerous rival, because they adopted a tolerant attitude towards it.

When first introduced to Japan, Christianity enjoyed the favor of the political authorities. As we have seen, Buddhism had become corrupt and almost entirely secular. Buddhist priests and their followers had become so powerful and obstreperous that Nobunaga considered them subversive elements in his campaign to unify Japan. He therefore opened war on Buddhism in general and, in 1571, burned and sacked the Tendai monasteries on Mount Hiei. He favored Christianity as a convenient rival to the influence of Buddhism, and he gave Christian missionaries a free hand. But a curious combination of circumstances soon led to the downfall of the Christian missions.

It was not long before the Buddhists perceived their error in tolerating Christianity and began a strong campaign to combat its influence. They could not stand idly by when they realized that Christians regarded all other religions as inferior and were intent upon evangelizing the whole of the nation. There was also considerable disfavor in official circles of the Catholic doctrine of allegiance to the pope in Rome. But it should be pointed out that there were other factors contributing to the rising anti-Christian sentiment for which the missionaries themselves could not be held responsible. The first Westerners to reach Japan had been Portuguese, and the first missionaries were Catholics. Dutch traders began to explore this new field of activity not much later, and, with their arrival, the foreign elements in Japan reflected the political and religious disputes which were at that time raging in Europe. The Japanese learned much of value from their European visitors in the way of science and took a great interest in medicine, astronomy, navigation, and mathematics, but they also learned that the conflicting ideologies of the West, if given a free hand, could mean further disorder in Japan. Hideyoshi and Ieyasu did not wish to harbor foreign controversies which could threaten their unification program; accordingly, they determined to suppress Christianity, having found it to be as disruptive an element as Buddhism.

In 1587, the propagation of Christianity was prohibited, and foreign missionaries were ordered to leave Japan. The order, however, was not enforced by local lords, and the missions continued to make progress. In 1597, the campaign to suppress Christianity began in earnest, and 26 missionaries and converts were crucified at Nagasaki. Real persecution followed. Death sentences were given to those who professed to be Christians and even to those who sheltered Christians. Many remained loyal to their religious convictions, but the Christian movement was paralyzed. Under Ieyasu, the persecution gathered force; under Iemitsu, the third Tokugawa shogun, Japan went through an anti-foreign phase which culminated in the severance of relations with foreign countries. The Dutch were given minor trading concessions, but, in 1640, all other foreigners were excluded, some Portugese envoys from Macao were beheaded, and Japan effectively isolated herself from the rest of the world.

Tokugawa Period and the Meiji Restoration

Japan enjoyed two and a half centuries of peace in the Tokugawa period (1615–1868). In the field of religion, however, there was a steady decline. Buddhism became the only religion recognized by the state. Certain sects obtained special favors from the government, particularly the Jodo sect of Amidaism, and many magnificent temples were built and supported by the state. But the relationship between the shogunate and the church was a peculiar one. The shoguns controlled the temples and the priesthood and used them in regimenting the social as well as the spiritual life of the people. Everyone was required to register at a temple as a Buddhist, and this register, originally designed to weed out Christians, came to serve many purposes. It was used as a census register. Births, marriages, changes of abode or employment, travels, and various other activities were recorded by the temples. Theirs was essentially a police function in the eyes of the state. Such regimentation of religious life naturally led to a further loss of spiritual vitality, and, although all subjects of the Japanese nation became Buddhists by decree, there was no corresponding revival of interest in the doctrines of the church.

There were philosophical developments outside Buddhism in this period, however, which were destined to play an important role later. Zen Buddhism, which lost much of its prestige with the rise of the Tokugawa shoguns, included Confucian doctrines in its teachings, and, while Zen was in its ascendancy, Confucian ethics and morality had become an important influence on the feudal system. The teachings of Shushi, a Chinese Confucian scholar of the twelfth century, were introduced by Zen priests and, in the seventeenth century, attracted wide interest among scholars. While the religious life of the nation was dominated by Buddhism, the practical ethics of the people and the philosophical basis for the feudal government in the Tokugawa period were founded on Confucian doctrine. Confucianism, however, was never organized as an independent religion.

Another important development in the early Tokugawa period was the rise of the Mito school of historians. Its members studied early Japanese texts and aroused public interest in the history of national literature and religions. The result was a growing resentment against the shogunate on the part of many influential people. For centuries the imperial family had remained in comparative obscurity, its emperors the mere pawns of ruling factions. The claims of the imperial dynasty were at last brought to the attention of the public, and many elements began to seek restoration of imperial rule. The most important factor in this movement was the resurrection of ancient texts which brought about a revival of interest in the dormant Shinto religion. The *Nihongi* was published with commentaries, and this eighth-century chronicle served in the nineteenth century to arouse great popular interest in the mythical "age of the gods." It cast an almost forgotten light on Japanese history, and its legends of divine origin were made a religious basis for the restoration of the emperor system.

The latter part of the Tokugawa period was unsettled. The dissatisfaction of the people with their government became increasingly marked. There were frequent minor rebellions and agrarian uprisings. The shogunate was almost bankrupt, and its hold on the reigns of government relaxed. Buddhism, the state religion, fell into disrepute, and its priests, content with the luxuries provided by wealthy patrons, ceased all active evangelism. As public interest in Shinto mounted, the Buddhists became the helpless butt of their Confucian and Shinto critics. In the early part of the nineteenth century, American vessels began to explore the Japanese coasts. By 1854, Commodore Perry had concluded a treaty with the shogunate which opened Japan to foreign intercourse and led to treaties with other nations. This renewed contact with foreign powers only served to increase the unrest in Japan. The country was divided into various factions. Eventually, the southern feudal lords, who had attained semi-independence due to the laxness of the central government, gathered their forces and opened a full-scale revolution with the intention of restoring imperial rule. In 1868, they forced the shogun to resign, abolished feudalism, placed the emperor on the throne, and made Tokyo the capital of the nation. Japan entered the Meiji period and the modern phase of her history.

At the close of the Tokugawa period, Buddhist prestige had reached its lowest ebb, but it was due for one more blow. Stimulated by government propaganda, antagonism to Buddhism mounted. Persecutions ensued in which many Buddhist temples were closed, their estates confiscated, and the priests compelled to abandon their posts. The tide of anti-Buddhist feeling ran high, but Buddhism was so deeply rooted in the tradition of the people that it slowly recovered much of its lost prestige. Christianity, which at first was forbidden by law, eventually succeeded in re-establishing itself with the help of diplomatic pressure. Although it suffered occasional periods of depression and popular disfavor, it gradually became a vital factor in the religious life of the nation. Various other religious bodies appeared in the course of the nineteenth century, most of them outgrowths of the revival of primitive Shinto. These flourished among the less-educated people of the nation. Today, they constitute perhaps the most active religious groups in Japan, despite their numerical inferiority to the older religions. They were classified for convenience by the government as sects of Shinto, although their connection with the primitive religion was often slight. And, over and above all these religious institutions, there was the officially-sponsored national cult of Shinto, which dated back to the Sun Goddess cult of the Yamato clan and proclaimed the divine origin of the Japanese race and its sovereign. This was not readily accepted by Japanese loyal to other religious persuasions, but, in the course of time, through its intimate connection with the imperial family and through propaganda and government decrees, it gained ascendancy over all other religious bodies, and its doctrines were accepted by all loyal Japanese as the fundamental basis for the Japanese state.

2

ROLE OF GOVERNMENT IN RELIGIOUS LIFE

Atttempts to Establish a Theocratic State

The ideological basis for the restoration of direct rule by the emperor was religious as well as political, for the loyalists who brought it about were inspired by renascent Shinto. The Meiji government lost no time in attempting to establish a theocratic state based on the supra-religious cult of Shinto. Some of the most drastic reforms of the Meiji Restoration concerned religion. From 1868 to the termination of hostilities in 1945, the development of religious institutions was so inextricably bound to government policies that only an examination of those policies will suffice to explain religious life in modern Japan.

One of the first things done when the emperor assumed control was to revive the Department of Shinto (*Jingi-kan*). At first, this was one of seven cabinet departments, but, in July, 1869, it was made independent of the cabinet. The Department of Shinto had cognizance over ceremonies and festivals, property matters, ranking of priests, rules for priests, regulations for shrines, study of parishioners, and regulations for grants to shrines. All but the first item were handled by means of cabinet ordinances. The government exerted every possible effort in its attempt to establish Shinto as the national religion. An imperial rescript was issued in 1870 defining the relation of Shinto to the state and clearly stating the intention of the government to establish a national cult based on worship of the Sun Goddess. In the same year, the government placed officials in charge of propaganda in each of the old feudatories and began an intensive program of systematic instruction in the nature of the unity of Shinto and the state (*saisei ichi*). But there was, surprisingly, a strong resistance to the government's policies both on the part of Buddhism and on the part of the new religious groups which had sprouted in the late days of the Tokugawa period.

Realizing its failure in the creation of a national religion, the government abolished the Department of Shinto in August, 1871. In its place was set up the Shinto Ministry (*Jingi-sho*), but this, too, survived only a short while, being abolished the following year. The government had set out on a policy of discrediting Buddhism and making Shinto the national cult, but had found to its dismay that the faith of the people was based on elements drawn without distinction from both Shinto and Buddhism. The anti-Buddhist movement caused so much confusion in the national psychology at a time when national unity was imperative that the government was forced to abandon its original plan and devise a means for accommodating both religions. Accordingly, a Religions Ministry (*Kyobu-sho*) was established in April, 1872, with jurisdiction over the affairs of both Buddhism and Shinto. Its function was primarily to guide the religions and morals of the people, and, in so doing, it had authority to regulate the affairs of sects, control the establishment of shrines and temples, fix the grades and ranks of shrines and temples and of their priests, appoint the priests of Shinto and Buddhism, and supervise religious doctrines. In short, religious activities came almost entirely under the jurisdiction of the government.

In May, 1872, an Administrative Office (*Kyodo-shoku*) was set up within the Religions Ministry to supervise the activities of religious teachers nominated by the government. These missionaries were appointed from both Shinto and Buddhist priesthoods and also included a number of actors and literary figures. They were intrusted with carrying out the government's program of cultural education. An indication of the lines along which the government was thinking is seen in the three principles which guided its propaganda. These were: (1) reverence for national deities shall be observed, (2) "the heavenly reason" and "the way of humanity" shall be promulgated, and (3) the throne shall be revered and the authorities obeyed.

The attempt to amalgamate Buddhism and Shinto was doomed to failure. The difficulties naturally inherent in an attempt to control and direct such diverse elements contributed much to this failure, but there was another factor working against the government's policies. There were repercussions from Japanese representatives in the Occident who were subjected to criticism for their government's intolerance. Separation of religion and the state was demanded since contact with the Occident made nominal adherence to religious freedom a necessity. As early as 1873, the edict banning Christianity was lifted in response to diplomatic pressure. In 1875, after it had become apparent that the Shinto-Buddhist federation could not succeed, an ordinance was issued prohibiting cooperative missionary work by Shinto and Buddhist priests. The step marked the end of the experiment in a dual state religion. Finally, in 1877, the Religions Ministry itself was disbanded.

The Administrative Office, which had been created in 1872, survived the dissolution of the Religions Ministry and continued to supervise religious affairs in an administrative capacity. But it was now faced by an unforeseen problem. The government policy of indoctrinating the people in the national cult of Shinto had given momentum to the various small cults of Shinto which had arisen in the first half of the nineteenth century. These gained wide popular support. Although they showed unmistakable Shinto characteristics, their doctrines contained variations sufficient to cause serious discrepancies with the doctrines of the officially-sponsored state religion. When it became obvious that efforts to control these sects of Shinto were doomed to failure, the government, in 1882, recognized them as independent religious bodies. Shinto was divided by law into Shrine Shinto and Sectarian Shinto. The sects were regarded as independent organizations which had to depend upon their constituents for support, while the shrines were supported officially by the state. In 1884, the Administrative Office was dissolved, making the legal separation of church and state complete. The government decreed that the national shrines were not religious institutions and prohibited all preaching and exhortations in the shrines. It abandoned its efforts to supervise officially the religious life of the nation and, henceforth, relied on Shrine Shinto for the development and support of a national cult.

Creation and Development of the Shrine Board

The main points of difference between the two forms of Shinto thus differentiated by governmental decrees were the following. Sectarian Shinto was based, for the most part, on the faith and activities of historical founders. Shrine Shinto, on the other hand, claimed to perpetuate the authentic and traditional beliefs and rituals of the Japanese race and declared that it had developed spontaneously in the national life without the aid of individual historical founders. The sects, like all other ordinary religious bodies, maintained their own independent organizations.

Their legal properties were totally distinct from those of the shrines. They were denied the use of the latter as meeting places. Except in special cases, they were not permitted to make use of the *torii*. On the other hand, shrines received supervision and a measure of financial support from the village, municipal, prefectural, or national government, depending on the grade of the particular shrine. Special legal enactments regulated the affairs of the shrines in matters of organization, priesthood, and ceremony. The activities of the shrines were limited to the celebration of ceremonies and festivals considered appropriate to the fostering of national characteristics.

This, however, was only a beginning, for the government now had nearly 200,000 shrines completely under its control. To develop these shrines into a "shrine system" was no mean task. It required an administrative organization, pyramided to the highest control in the country, and an ideology to bind it together.

The unifying ideology was supplied by the Imperial Rescript on Education promulgated in 1890 and by supplementary and supporting ordinances. The rescript exalts loyalty to the emperor and enjoins respect for the "way of the gods." No other document was ever treated with greater reverence. Prohibition of religious instruction in schools and the development of definite techniques of reverence for the emperor and national deities, such as shrine attendance and obeisance before the imperial portrait, were a part of the program. The rescript was regarded as limited to schools and students, but it was a pattern for the entire nation.

The methods employed by the government in the supervision of shrines are of interest. By a system of gradation from local communities up through towns, cities, prefectures, and the Home Ministry, a complete network was established. Every phase of shrine activity was controlled. Shrines were state institutions in almost every respect. It is a mistake, however, to regard any of the shrines as entirely government-supported, for the grants were seldom more than tokens of support. Government sponsorship, however, resulted in stimulation of shrine worship which resulted in more gifts, and government officials decided the amounts to be raised through local neighborhood associations in what might be called extra-legal taxes.

Since the shrines were only under the supervision of a bureau in the Home Ministry, ultranationalists felt that the dignity of the gods was being insulted. They continued to work for the establishment of a Department of Shinto directly under the emperor.

In April, 1900, shrines and religions were put in separate bureaus. No further agitation occurred until 1913, at which time the Religions Bureau was transferred to the Education Ministry. Recommendations for the creation of a Shrine Board were also made in 1923, but no action resulted.

In 1935, members of the Shrine Investigation Committee asked for a separate board. The arguments they advanced are interesting: "(1) The divine will of our imperial ancestors is not being followed by the present Shrine Bureau; (2) a special board is necessary in order to enlighten and lead the nation; and (3) the quality of leadership and activity of the present bureau is inadequate."

As the war fever mounted, agitation increased until, in 1939, a decision was reached to establish a separate board under the Home Ministry, and in the following year the Shrine Board (*Jingi-in*) was actually established. The creation of this board, however, was not a complete triumph for the national-cult school since the board was still under the Home Ministry. The ultimate goal was a national cult board directly under the emperor as the high priest of the nation.

Control of Religion

Contact with Occidental nations and the necessity of admitting Christianity deterred, but did not discourage, efforts to control religion. The constitution promulgated in 1889 paid lip service to religious freedom in Article 28, which stated:

"Japanese subjects shall, within limits not prejudicial to peace and order, and not antagonistic to their duties as subjects, enjoy freedom of religious belief."

This provision gave hope to advocates of religious freedom and was constantly mentioned in propaganda abroad. "There has to be religious freedom," people were told, "because it is in the Constitution."

Efforts to revive control of religions by means of a religions bill went on quietly for four decades. These efforts never resulted in complete success from a legal standpoint. The power of religious sects was sufficient to prevent absolute control of religion, such as was envisaged in the days of the Restoration, but the sects could not prevent control of religious organizations. Even the Religious Bodies Law, promulgated in 1939 and enforced from April 1, 1940, was not as strict as its supporters desired. The Diet introduced certain modifications. The Education Ministry, however, was equal to the situation. Where it seemed desirable, the Ministry withdrew the objectionable items for later issuance as departmental regulations so that the law would pass the Diet.

The Religious Bodies Law gave the Minister of Education, and through him, the governors and local officials, supervisory responsibility in all matters of organization, personnel, activities, and teaching. It compelled all sects to concentrate responsibility in the hands of a leader, who could not assume office until his election had been approved by a competent official and who could not resign until a successor had received approval. Through the power of the Education Minister and the prefectural governors, the government was able to maintain complete control over religion. It is not without significance that the establishment of the Shrine Board was postponed until the Religious Bodies Law was promulgated.

The totalitarian pattern toward which the country was rapidly moving in the late 1930's included the regimentation of religion. The instrument for achieving this was the Religious Bodies Law, which placed religious affairs once more in the hands of the government. With the dawn of 1941, the ultra-nationalists were nearing their goal. Union was forced upon the various sects of Buddhism and Christianity. A Religions League, composed of Christian, Buddhist, and Sectarian Shinto Federations, was organized. The machinery for utilizing religion for totalitarian ends was complete.

Religious Organizations and the Government

Under the provisions of the Religious Bodies Law, religious organizations had the status of legal persons. In order to found a new sect, application had to be filed with the Minister of Education, who had final jurisdiction over all religions. The application covered rules, regulations, creed, doctrines, methods of propaganda, and social work. Already established sects had to be re-registered and had to report all the details required of new sects. Subsequent changes required the approval of the Minister of Education.

The establishment of temples, churches, and shrines and all subsequent changes required the approval of the prefectural governor, who was given jurisdiction over matters of personnel, doctrine, and finance.

Within sects and denominations, changes in regulations required the approval of the organization's head and of the representatives of the believers. The head of each organization was given almost dictatorial powers over his organization but was held responsible by the government for all acts of the organization. It was intended that the representatives of believers would protect the local congregations from exploitation or manipulation by their leaders. Local bodies not wishing to join a national organization were permitted to become "associations" under the governors, which in reality meant local police supervision. Sects and local organizations could be disbanded at the discretion of the Minister of Education or the competent local official.

There were many provisions regarding personnel, taxes, reports, and disciplinary or punitive measures. All in all, the Religious Bodies Law provided the government with the machinery for complete and immediately effective control of any religious organization or leader. It was said to be designed not to control religious organization but to facilitate mobilization of the national spirit. Organizations that cooperated in this mobilization and modified their teachings and activities according to official desires had no cause for anxiety. As long as they accepted official dictation, their activities were free from government interference. This was prewar Japan's interpretation of religious freedom.

The Religious Bodies Law was greeted with apprehension on the part of some, but, on the whole, the reception was favorable. The heightened national tensions caused all to lose perspective, and even many Christians took occasion to acclaim the enactment of the law because of the official recognition it accorded Christianity.

The manner in which the law was enforced soon removed any doubts as to what was intended. Every item of the regulations was scrutinized with the greatest care by government officials.

Church officials were constantly running back and forth between the Ministry of Education and their headquarters, seeking for approval to make modifications required by the government. Great pressure was exerted on Buddhist, Shinto, and Christian sects to unite and, in certain cases, to eliminate parts of their scriptures and teachings. This goal of the government was never fully achieved. Certain Buddhist and Shinto sects resisted and successfully maintained their separate existence. The majority of Protestant Christians formed the Church of Christ in Japan. The Catholic Church was the only other recognized Christian body. The Osaka Diocese and a few scattered congregations of the Episcopal Church joined the Church of Christ in Japan, but the main body broke up into separate congregations. The Japan Orthodox Church was never recognized. Christian groups had the problem of severing relationship with foreign missionaries and churches. In the end, complete financial and political autonomy from foreign churches was achieved.

This change was not accomplished in an atmosphere of calm deliberation. The psychological regimentation of religion had been proceeding slowly during the decade of the so-called "national emergency," which began with the invasion of Manchuria in 1931. In the summer of 1940, however, a new situation arose. The Yonai Cabinet fell in July, and the second Konoye Cabinet, with its "new structure" slogan, turned the political, social, and economic world of Japan into turmoil. The "new structure" in religion meant, among other things, independence from foreign assistance. The Episcopal Church and the Salvation Army were especially vulnerable and so became objects of vicious attacks. A spy scare was promoted all summer and fall. When the Axis Treaty was signed in September, there were numerous arrests of foreigners. In October, the American Government advised all Americans not engaged in important duties to withdraw from

Japan. There had been a gradual shrinkage in the numbers of Protestant missionaries throughout the decade, but now a definite exodus of all Americans began in the fall. It was in such an atmosphere that the Protestants gathered on October 17, 1940, to celebrate the 2600th anniversary of the founding of Japan and issued a manifesto declaring their intention to form a united church. The situation was difficult, and Christian leaders believed the existence of Christianity in Japan was at stake.

The relationship between religious organizations and the state throughout the modern era had been one of paternalistic guidance. The government went as far as it could in securing the cooperation of religion in state policies, and it manipulated public opinion, through the press and patriotic societies, in order to create social as well as political pressure on religious bodies. On the other hand, pressure was brought to bear by patriotic societies on political, religious, and governmental bodies. Where officials lacked zeal for nationalism, they were urged to action. If they failed to carry out the wishes of those promoting national expansion, they were purged. These forces were brought into focus by the Religious Bodies Law.

Militarism in Religion, 1931-1941

Long before 1940, religious bodies were being utilized to enhance nationalism and militarism. Shrines, local and national, took on added prestige. Worship at shrines was not merely an indication of enthusiasm for the military, it was a test of being a true Japanese subject. In the early decades of the modern era, Christians remained aloof from shrine worship, but, in 1940, they participated fully, even to the extent of sending representatives to report at Ise Shrine regarding ecclesiastical activities. For some time, the Catholic Church refused to participate in shrine worship, but, finally, on the basis of the government's declaration that shrines were not religious, permission was given, and "shrine obeisance" by Catholic bodies became common. Only a few Christian groups refused to participate in such worship. The others permitted themselves to drift with the nationalistic current flowing so strongly through Japanese life.

It is difficult to single out any one type of shrine as being peculiarly given to ultranationalistic or militaristic tendencies. All shrines became instrumental in furthering national aims, for their priests were government officials and, as such, were under orders from the local or national government offices. The Ise, Kashiwara, and Meiji Shrines were centers of ultranationalistic Mikadoism. Yasukuni and the Gokoku shrines fostered the war spirit by exaltation of sacrifice on the field of battle. The Hachiman shrines, because of their association with the war god, became unusually popular.

Buddhists were also active in the promotion of militarism and nationalistic expansion. Collections were made for the purchase of airplanes. Ultranationalistic movies were promoted by Buddhist organizations. Nichiren priests attained a special reputation for chauvinism. Certain temples appear to have been rendezvous for some of the most ultranationalistic schemers. Of far greater significance were patriotic societies which were devoted to achieving a combination of the "imperial way" and Buddhist doctrines.

Religious organizations, like all other societies in Japan, were expected to participate in what was known as the "Spiritual Mobilization Movement." Special groups performed their assigned functions such as preparing comfort kits, going to stations to send off soldiers, sending messengers or speakers to camps, and caring for the families of soldiers. These were the normal duties of any patriotic society; they were accepted by all religious bodies. Unique in the Japanese scene is the emphasis on the national cult of Shinto. There were Buddhists, Sectarian Shintoists, and Christians who hesitated to go the full length of placing the emperor, the Sun Goddess, and worship of the Shinto pantheon above their personal faith, but the vast majority did as they were told, even though they may have had some mental reservations.

Japan was at war for virtually the entire period from September 18, 1931, when Japanese troops drove Chang Hsui Liang from Manchuria, until August 15, 1945. The unification and utilization of religions was only a preliminary to the supreme effort which began with war against the United States and Great Britain. Religious bodies had been sufficiently disciplined by then so that there was no question about their co-operating. What the world was not prepared for was their almost complete submission to the state in matters of theology and worship as well as in patriotic service. For, during the years from 1941 to 1945, religion was the almost completely subservient handmaiden of the state.

Militarism in Religion, 1941-1945

Imperial rescripts, especially the Rescript on Education, were always treated as holy writ, but their use was reserved for special occasions of significance. With the opening of the Pacific phase of the war, the rescript announcing the state of war was read in connection with almost all public occasions, including Christian Sunday worship and communion services. This was part of a service known as "the people's ceremony" and included bowing toward the palace and singing the national anthem. Money for war planes was raised by practically all religious bodies, and certain religious organizations even had their names attached to the planes. The members of religious bodies were organized into patriotic associations with their religious leaders as chairmen. These organizations were developed on prefectural and national levels under the leadership of prefectural governors.

Many religious institutions were taken over by the military, and their followers, absorbed in special patriotic activities, had little time left for the spiritual. Victory celebrations were sometimes arranged by joint action of Buddhists, Shintoists, and Christians; sometimes they were held separately. When a celebration fell on Sunday, observance was made a part of Christian church services. Prayers for victory were composed by leaders of the three religions. The 16,000 Shinto priests were ordered to exert themselves specially in this regard.

On August 28, 1944, the Home Ministry issued instructions to Shinto priests as follows: "The war has entered an important phase. You, servants of the deities, must devote yourselves to your duty more and more. With sincerity, pray for the conquest of the haughty enemy."

At the same time, the Vice-President of the Shrine Board sent the following instructions to prefectural governors: "You are requested to see that the priests under your jurisdiction observe the purport of the instruction and devote themselves to their duty still more in order to leave nothing to be desired in their service to the deities. You are requested, at this juncture, to take appropriate steps regarding conditions in your respective jurisdictions in order to make people pray for the conquest of the enemy, feel the august virtue of the deities, entertain strong faith in our victory, and affirm still more their resolution to guard the imperial country."

Ideology and ritual suffered along with the organization and activity of the sects. Religious bodies were expected to modify their teachings so as to incorporate the idea of "the imperial way." Constitutions, creeds, catechisms, and hymnals of all religious bodies were scrutinized and modified. Some had to make fewer changes than others. Adjustment of theology to Shinto mythology was urged upon all bodies. Response to this varied, and certain adjustments were still in progress at the time of the surrender.

In promoting the "holy war," religious leaders were called upon to go to the conquered countries and make contacts with those of similar faith. Under military sponsorship, religious organizations identical with those in Japan were promoted by these representatives.

The ceremonies for the deification of war dead at Yasukuni and at the prefectural Gokoku shrines provided moments of intense emotional experience for the bereaved. They also served as festivals for the development of the war spirit. On either side of the long approach at Yasukuni Shrine, there were large animated pictures depicting famous land and sea victories. Each day, at 4 A.M. and 8 A.M., special prayers for victory were offered by Yasukuni priests.

While it is true that the overwhelming influence of religion was exerted on the side of ultranationalism and militarism, the few who refused to collaborate with the militarists should not be ignored. No study has been made of the number who were imprisoned or suffered because of non-cooperation or opposition. Some, however, who took such attitudes escaped molestation entirely. Early in the Manchurian affair, a Christian pastor published in his magazine an article in which he declared that Japan was like a rich man demanding the property of his poorer neighbors. There were a number of pastors who staunchly refused to participate in or sanction shrine worship. Probably a few hundred pastors and priests were imprisoned because of their faith and "non-co-operation." Some of these died in prison or soon after being freed. The Holiness and Seventh Day Adventist churches, which persisted in proclaiming God as King of Kings and Lord of Lords and emphasized the certainty of the final judgment, were suppressed, and their leaders were imprisoned. Uncooperative Buddhist priests were intimidated into silence. Some sects refused to acquiesce in extreme demands to have their scriptures purged of objectionable passages. It is reported that at least one Buddhist sect contributed ambulances but declined to raise money for planes. Local efforts to install family altars or god-shelves were successfully resisted by most Christians and by some Buddhists. Perhaps note should also be taken of the fact that many religious workers apparently carried on their ministrations and quietly ignored demands which the prominent leaders could not escape. There are no records of recantation in favor of Shintoism, and only a very small number of Christian pastors repudiated their faith.

For the Japanese people in general, however, the war itself was a religious experience. The nation was stirred up to a state of fanatical zeal based on a sense of national destiny centering in the divine nature of the emperor and the sacred "national structure." The idea of a "divine wind" (*kamikaze*) seemed no idle dream for the masses. The impossible was happening: Japan was challenging the world. History had reached one of its major crises. In this mood, Christians, Buddhists, and Shintoists alike were carried on an emotional wave which swept away the foundations of reason and religion. Subservience to "the way of the gods" and "the imperial way" was inevitable.

Postwar Adjustments

During the war the three recognized religions were organized in the "Great Japan Wartime Religious Patriotic Association," an organization subsidized by the government and headed by the Minister of Education. Its name expresses its purpose.

A few weeks after the surrender, this patriotic association was changed into the Religions League, and the Buddhist, Shinto, and Christian Bureaus became cooperating federations. When the Shrine Association was organized, it also joined. All leadership by government officials ceased, but so far as the religions themselves were concerned, wartime leadership remained largely unchanged.

The Religions League was organized on a national, prefectural, and, in some cases, a local level. Briefly, its activities were as follows: liaison with the government and with other organizations, liaison with the Occupation, establishment and extension of religious culture, promotion of interest in religion, promotion of peace sentiment and international good will, publication of religious literature, and research activities.

In October, 1945, a small Religious Affairs Section was organized in the Bureau of Social Education of the Ministry of Education. In April, 1946, it was transferred to the Minister's Secretariat where it remained. Location in the secretariat signalized its removal from the field of policy-making and indoctrination. Its functions were given as the protection of religious freedom under the constitution, registration of religious corporations, the making of surveys, and the maintenance of accurate statistics and records on religions and religious matters.

3

BUDDHISM: ORIGIN AND NATURE

Buddhism was founded by the Indian teacher and reformer, S'akyamuni Gautama (566–486 B.C.). The dominant religion of his day was Brahmanism, which consisted principally in the recitation of holy texts, the performances of traditional rites, and meditation on philosophical problems. The Brahmans and certain ascetics among them believed that every mortal is destined to be reborn through a transmigration cycle in a station commensurate with the merits or demerits accumulated during his lifetime. The ascetics, however, also believed a person could escape the transmigration cycle and attain a state of perfect tranquility, or nirvana, by realizing the "truth" through certain physical and mental exercises. And it was these ideas in modified form which became the essential elements of S'akyamuni's philosophy.

S'akyamuni was the son of an influential lord of the S'akya clan who, forsaking his wordly life, devoted himself to asceticism and, after many years of self-mortification, became convinced that he was a Buddha, or Enlightened One. He resolved to make known the way to the truth he had found and gathered followers around him, who either joined his order or became devout laymen. His public activities lasted 45 years, and, when he died at the age of 80, his teachings had already gained considerable popularity in the Ganges Valley.

S'akyamuni's teachings were memorized by his disciples and were later compiled in the form of sutras, or scriptures. These now appear in several languages. They have acquired so many philosophical accretions that it is difficult to ascertain what was actually taught by him and what is simply credited to him. Apparently he preached that happiness and salvation come from within, that all phenomena are transitory, that life itself is the root of all imperfection and sorrow, and that the extinction of desire enables a man to attain salvation. By salvation, he meant the attainment of a state of nirvana—a state of perpetual enlightenment or perfect bliss. S'akyamuni regarded morality, meditation, and intuition as the proper approach to the "truth"; for the attainment of salvation, he recommended four steps: (1) realization of the plight of human beings, (2) examination into the causes of the plight, (3) annihilation of these causes, and (4) practice of the "way."

As Buddhism spread over India, sectarian differences appeared and two major divisions developed. One division, later known as Southern or Hinayana Buddhism, stressed the teachings of the founder and sought to preserve them in as pure a form as possible. It spread south to Ceylon and east through Burma, French Indo-China, and Siam to Malaya. The other division, known as Northern or Mahayana Buddhism, was essentially an elaboration of the founder's teachings and exhibited a tendency to compromise with foreign beliefs. It spread north into Central Asia and China and there it absorbed Taoist and Confucian teachings and produced further sectarian differences. A thousand years had passed since the days of the founder when this Mahayana Buddhism reached Japan in the sixth century of the Christian era. The Buddhism which was introduced into Japan contained philosophical modifications and theistic accretions and rituals totally unknown to primitive Buddhism. These fundamentally changed its original character in several important respects.

While it is impossible to determine its exact nature, the Buddhism which was first introduced into Japan contained Confucian doctrines on practical ethics, traces of Taoist dualism, and an elaborate pantheon of deities. In short, Buddhism through the centuries had absorbed so many foreign philosophies and had split into so many schools and sects that it in no way represented a unified body of religious opinion. Since Japan fell heir from the very beginning to these often-contradictory sectarian differences, it is little wonder that Japanese Buddhism never resembled the religion of the original Buddha. The Japanese themselves eventually modified Buddhism and adapted it to Japanese culture so successfully that an indigenous Buddhism evolved, which differs radically from the Buddhism of both China and India.

The early sects of Buddhism established during the Nara period were strictly Chinese transplantations employing Chinese architecture, costumes, rites, and language. With the passage of time and the opening of the Heian period, however, two outstanding sects—Tendai and Shingon—were founded by Japanese scholars. While these borrowed extensively from parent organizations on the continent, they wisely compromised with the native Japanese religion so that they represented departures from Chinese tradition. Finally, as Buddhism was fading in India, the land of its origin, Japan produced a truly indigenous Buddhism in the Kamakura period. The great spiritual awakening of the twelfth and thirteenth centuries which saw the rise of Amidaism, Zen, and Nichirenism produced a distinctly Japanese Buddhism.

While some of the earliest sects have disappeared and many subdivisions have been formed within the larger sects, no major division or significant movement had taken place during the last seven centuries. After the Restoration of 1868, there were many efforts to adapt Buddhism to the modern world and to cushion it from the impact of Christianity, Western science, and the revived Shinto. But, while it was profoundly affected by science and Western thought, no outstanding new sects appeared. The Religious Bodies Law of 1939 helped to reduce the number of minor sects. Since the end of the recent war and the establishment of religious freedom, however, nearly all sects have been disturbed by the grouping and re-grouping of sects, subsects, and orders. Though there appears to be a determined effort on the part of Buddhist leaders to unify and strengthen the whole body of the church, it is yet too early to predict the direction which Japanese Buddhism will take.

The Western mind, reared in the atmosphere of Christian or Jewish theology, will be puzzled if it approaches Buddhism with the expectation of finding in it something familiar. Pure Buddhism has practically no theology; it is basically a philosophy and must be so studied. Even as a philosophy, there is no uniformity or common pattern. Japanese Buddhism is a conglomerate of so many conflicting systems that it is as confusing as contemporary Christianity, with its Coptic, Greek Orthodox, Roman Catholic, and Protestant churches. There are, however, some elements common to the teachings of most sects, such as acceptance of S'akyamuni Gautama as the founder of Buddhism, acknowledgement of his teachings as the essence of truth, conception of the attainment of Buddhahood as salvation, belief in the "three precious things"—Buddha, the law, and the church— which S'akyamuni handed down to his followers, and belief in the three basic paths—morality, meditation, and intuition—as the proper approach to truth.

Few of these basic agreements will bear close scrutiny, for in detailed analysis they exhibit a wide variety of interpretations. Even Buddhist morality, which was originally legalistic, being defined in terms of five fundamental prohibitions—stealing, killing, lying, drinking, and adultery—has been highly colored by Confucian practical ethics. There are even many distinctly different conceptions of Buddha: there is the historical Buddha, or S'akyamuni himself; there are the mythical Buddhas of compassion, among whom Amida is the central figure; and there are the cosmic Buddhas, among whom Dainichi is the central figure. In addition to these prominent Buddhas, there are numberless lesser Buddhas and Buddhas-to-be called Bodhisattvas. A Buddhist generally seeks salvation, depending on his sectarian affiliations, by following "the way" revealed by S'akyamuni, by obtaining the favor of the mythical Buddha Amida, or by apprehending "universal truth" and realizing the fundamental identity between himself and the cosmic Buddha Dainichi. Beyond these basic doctrines lies a maze of unrelated sectarian interpretations, speculations, and mystic rituals.

4

BUDDHISM : INSTITUTIONAL ASPECTS

Buddhism in Japan is an institution as well as a philosophy, and, as an institution, it has certain characteristics which hold true regardless of sectarian differences. It has a priesthood, possesses scriptures, conducts services, maintains temples, large estates, and schools, and engages in social welfare activities. It is organized into sects with millions of followers and is a force behind social and political movements.

Sect Organization

Buddhist schools, sects, or sub-sects are usually started by a leader who establishes himself in a center—perhaps a small hermitage—where he gathers disciples and followers. As disciples spread his teachings, their missionary outposts become branch temples and the original center becomes the headquarters, or main temple. Branch temples are usually smaller than the main temple, but this is not always the case. One of these may, in turn, develop a satellite which regards the branch temple as its headquarters, and this process can continue to the fourth or even fifth degree. When this happens, the original center often becomes a grand head temple, the secondary center becomes a great head temple. Small preaching centers with congregations are known as chapels.

49

The whole complex body of such an institution is usually called a sect. When the founder dies, there frequently develop conflicting interpretations of his teachings. Various branches appear within the doctrinal framework of the original sect when this happens. These, in time, become administratively independent and may assume different names although they only represent variations of one school of thought. As they grow increasingly powerful and more divergent in their interpretations, they take on the aspect of sects. Thus, the original sect from which they all stemmed is regarded as a school of Buddhism while its offshoots are called sects of that particular school. And, within each branch or new sect, there are often orders and minor groups which never become administratively independent.

Sects, as a rule, divide leadership responsibility between two offices, that of a spiritual leader and that of an administrative leader. In most cases, both of these offices are held concurrently by the same man, who may also be the chief abbot of a head temple. Administrative problems have always been nominally entrusted to various committees and boards, but, until recently, decisions on all spiritual affairs and on many temporal matters were made by the spiritual leaders. The intricacies of sectarian politics often made the spiritual leaders the mere pawn of sectarian bosses, whose power and influence was tremendous when decisions affected millions of adherents and vast property holdings. Due to postwar changes, this authority has been restricted considerably, and the burden of responsibility is now carried by advisory councils and sect assemblies. The reduction of income from estates, the increased dependence on assessments, and the danger of secession has caused the influence of local temple representatives on the policies of sect headquarters to become an increasingly important factor, although many conservatives still cling to the old administrative organizations.

The Priesthood

In primitive Buddhism there were four ecclesiastical orders: monks, nuns, devout laymen, and devout laywomen. Monks and nuns, having forsaken the world, devoted themselves to religious practices. Those who were unable to do this became laymen. They observed the specified commandments and supported Buddhism by contributing buildings, clothing, and food. By living a moral life and by giving alms, they hoped to accumulate merit and attain salvation in some future existence. In Mahayana Buddhism, the role of laymen became increasingly important and Bodhisattvas were generally represented as laymen.

As Buddhism advanced northward, its monastic system became more and more relaxed. Followers outside India paid more attention to doctrinal matters than to discipline, and literal observances of certain commandments established in India became impossible because of the climate. The administration of the church also changed. In Indian monasteries, some monks managed the administration of their institution but had no privilege, being considered inferior to those completely absorbed in religious practices. In China, however, it became necessary to appoint monks to act as officials in charge of other monks. They were given titles and were the forerunners of high priests.

When Buddhism was introduced to Japan, the government established three titles for priest-officials after the Chinese pattern. Priests within these categories were further divided by a system of ranks. All who wished to become priests had to obtain permission from the government. However, in the Heian period and thereafter, these titles were bestowed on priests without implication of official position. Thus, an extremely complicated heirarchy developed. Some centuries later, in 1873, the Meiji government abolished government control of church titles, permitting each

51

sect to develop its own hierarchy. Today, there is no uniformity among different Buddhist sects in the titles and ranks of the priesthood. Most sects have three orders of priests with rank and one order of priests without rank. The latter are monks and are divided into two classes; some remain priests without rank throughout their lifetime and are not entitled to become chief priests of temples; others, if they have had considerable education, can in time enter the ranks of the priesthood. The role played by laymen in Indian Buddhism was completely transformed in Japan. The Tokugawa government required all citizens to register at Buddhist temples and become active members of the church, but this regulation served only to create a formal and unsubstantial relationship between the temples and their laymen. Because of this tradition, most Japanese even today, while nominally Buddhist supporters, are generally indifferent to the religious matters of the church.

The list of titles and ranks given below is that for the priesthood of the Shingon sect. The English term used as equivalents of these ranks are chiefly those of the Roman Catholic Church, which most nearly approximate those of this typical Buddhist organization; they should not be accepted as literal translations since no exact equivalents exist in the English language.

Archbishop.... (*Daisojo*) ⎱
Bishop.... (*Sojo*) ⎰ .... 6 grades
Ranking Priests.... (*Sozu*) .... 6 grades
Priests.... (*Risshi*) .... 2 grades
Monks.... (*Soryo*) .... Priests without rank
Seminarians.... (*Kyoshi Shiho*) ...... Candidates for priesthood

Hereditary priesthood has been common since the beginning of the Meiji era. Usually, it is the eldest son of the chief priest of a temple who takes charge when his father retires for reasons of health or dies, but this is not always the case. Many men join the priesthood because of poverty or love of learning and rise to high positions.

The training of a priest differs with each sect, but, generally the preparation for priesthood begins at an early age. A young boy just finishing elementary school at the age of 12 or 13 registers at his father's temple as a monk. He continues to attend middle school and then enters a special seminary under the management of his sect. During his school years, he assists in services as an assistant priest, and, after graduation from the seminary, he may be appointed chief priest of some small temple. Every sect has a different system for grading its priests, some sects having as many as 15 grades. Promotion from one grade to another is not on the basis of merit but is more or less automatic. It is customary for promotion to be arranged through a fee paid to sect headquarters. This fee is willingly paid by recipients of the honor since a certain prestige comes with a higher grade. Because the more important and wealthier temples require a priest of a given rank, the achievement of high rank is looked upon as the means of becoming chief priest of such temples.

Rank is outwardly evident in the color of the robes worn by priests. Common monks wear black, bishops wear purple, and dark red is for archbishops only. The colors worn by intermediate ranks vary according to the sect.

Temples

In Japan the word "temple" is invariably used to indicate a Buddhist sanctuary. However, in its broadest sense, it can mean a whole institution and include many sanctuaries, lecture halls, schools, and dwellings.

A Japanese Buddhist temple is almost always built within an enclosure. At the entrance of most large temples, there is an imposing two-story gate which is painted red. Two huge doors block the entrance, but these are left open by day and are only closed at night. On each side of the entrance passageway stands a forbidding statue with scowling face, distorted eyes, and a threatening attitude. These represent two mythological kings who guard all temples from evil, and they are often covered with wads of paper. It is customary for worshippers to write prayers on small bits of paper, masticate them thoroughly, and throw them at these protective kings with the understanding that, if they stick to the images, the prayers will be answered.

Just inside the gates of the larger temples, there is usually a large, exposed bell which hangs from a simple roof supported only by four pillars. A heavy striking beam hangs horizontally beside the bell and is pulled away from it by means of a rope. The bell is rung when the released beam swings back against it. Smaller temples have a miniature bell hanging either in the entrance of the main sanctuary or inside the sanctuary.

Another distinctive feature of a Buddhist enclosure is the pagoda. The pagoda is a tall, narrow structure three or five stories high. Each floor level is surrounded by an apron of roof with upcurled ridges. The structure tapers off into a pyramidal roof surmounted by a tall finial spire. Pagodas are often elaborately ornamented.

The main sanctuary is called the Buddha Hall. It is generally the most imposing structure in the temple precincts, having a long, sloping roof with gently curled ridges, prominent supporting columns, and usually a quantity of decorative carvings and figures along its facade. The interior is plainly furnished and only dimly lighted by candles around the altar. Images of Buddhas, Bodhisattvas, lesser deities, and high priests can be discerned in the worship hall, and, around the altar, there are little bells placed on cushions and lacquer boxes containing scrolls of sutras. Lighted sticks of fragrant incense lend an aura of holiness to the atmosphere.

In addition to the above, there are within the compound many other buildings and appurtenances which characterize the various sects of Buddhism. The number and type of the buildings depend solely on the wealth and importance of the temple. Around the precincts are scattered a number of lesser objects such as stone dogs or lions, an ablution basin, a stupa, and perhaps a gong or drum. The stupa, originally a memorial to Buddha, is an imposing structure with a dome capped by a series of diminishing flat rings topped by a ring mounted vertically. The dome and pinnacle are symbolic of Buddha's bones. But few temples can afford a real stupa and substitute for it a small stone pillar three to five feet high. This is composed of five shapes—a sphere with a pointed tip, a crescent, a pyramid, a sphere, and a cube—which represent the five elements (space, air, fire, water, and earth). On all four sides, there are usually scriptures in Chinese, Sanskrit, and Japanese.

Burial grounds are often located in or adjacent to temple enclosures. These are usually quite extensive since burial services were a monopoly of Buddhism during the shogunate and almost a monopoly throughout the Meiji era. Within the burial grounds, one finds miniature stupas of stone or wood, but the wood stupas are sometimes little more than notched sticks.

Scriptures, Sacred Utensils, and Services

There is no fixed canon of scriptures in Buddhism. S'akyamuni's teachings have been preserved in a great variety of languages and forms. To these have been added many interpretations and foreign doctrines which are the basis for numerous sectarian differences. Hinayana Buddhism is based on the Pali sutras, which are probably the oldest and most authentic of the scriptures, but Japanese Buddhism is founded almost exclusively on the Chinese canon of Mahayana Buddhism. No one sect uses this canon in its entirety but all respect it. A sect usually limits its canon to certain sutras; some sects base their doctrines principally on only one or a part of one sutra. All temples have copies of the sutras recognized by the canon of their particular sects, and these are usually kept in a red lacquer box placed before the altar.

The objects of reverence and the sacred utensils depend on the nature of the sect, but, at every altar, there are images, small or large, elaborate or plain, on which worshippers focus their attention. The central figure at the altar is usually the main object of worship. This may be a statue of S'akyamuni, Dainichi, Amida, or some other Buddha, depending on the sect. An image of the founder of the sect is usually present and often a number of saints are venerated. Some sects even place a statue of the founder in the central position, giving it the appearance of the chief object of worship, as is the case with the Nichiren sect. Buddhist altars are almost always highly colored, gold usually, predominating. Around the altar are many smaller sacred objects, ornaments, and symbols. These vary greatly according to the sect, and there are some instances in which Shinto and even Christian symbols can be recognized. The sutras enclosed in their lacquer boxes and placed before the altars are naturally accorded great reverence and are handled only by priests.

There are no Buddhist services such as are common to the Christian world where congregations assemble at specified hours for communal worship. Daily, and at regular intervals, priests conduct services of adoration and worship, the nature of which again depends largely on the sect. Ordinarily, the sutras are chanted and prayers are offered. At such services, drums are sometimes beaten, bells are tinkled, and incense is burned. Worshippers, however, are not necessarily expected to attend these services. Rather, it is customary for the believers to present themselves at the temple at any convenient time to offer their prayers and engage in individual worship. There are certain Buddhist celebrations to which the devout laymen come en masse, but these are more in the nature of festivals. Special services to cure illness or to accomplish some desired end are occasionally held by request, but by far the most frequent services conducted by the Buddhist church are memorial services and funerals. Since the war, preaching has become more common.

5

BUDDHISM: DESCRIPTION OF SECTS

There are, at present, six major groups according to which all Japanese Buddhist sects can be classified: Nara, Tendai, Shingon, Amida, Zen, and Nichiren. As explained previously, these larger divisions should be regarded as schools of thought rather than sects, as they themselves are usually divided into sects which are loosely related through basically similar doctrines. Amida Buddhism, for instance, includes five major sects, one of which is divided into ten branches. On the other hand, the Nara sects are grouped solely by historical period, their doctrines being somewhat dissimilar. For the sake of simplicity, however, it is convenient to divide Japanese Buddhism into the six groups listed above.

Amida Buddhism is by far the most powerful influence in the Buddhist world of Japan and owes its strength to the great appeal and simplicity of its doctrine of salvation through the power of Amida. Zen Buddhism, with a wealth of historical and cultural tradition behind it, is second in number of adherents, followed closely by Shingon with its great appeal through esoteric mysteries. Nichirenism, though not so impressive numerically as these three, is nevertheless a vital force in Buddhism and exerts an influence comparable to theirs because of its fanaticism. The Tendai school which served as the fountainhead of Amidaism, Zen, and Nichirenism still has strong support but lacks vitality.

The Nara sects, though of historical significance, are now almost completely insignificant as factors in Japanese religious life.

The best available statistics place the number of Buddhists in Japan at roughly 43,000,000.

The Nara Sects

It is not known what sort of Buddhism was first brought to Japan in 552. It is clear, however, that real sectarian differences did not appear for more than 70 years. Buddhist missionaries from China realized that the Japanese were not yet prepared intellectually for sectarian speculations and wisely limited their teaching to general tenets and moral doctrines common to all Buddhism. It was not until the early part of the seventh century that real sectarian differentiation occurred.

Six sects were introduced from China between the years 625 and 754. Although Nara, the first real city in Japan, did not become the capital until 710, these sects are usually referred to as the Nara sects, because they reached their highest development and greatest influence in the Nara period (710–794). The Nara sects include the Sanron (625), Jojitsu (625), Hosso (654), Kusha (658), Kegon (736), and Ritsu (754) sects.

These early Buddhist sects in Japan employed Chinese architecture, costumes, and rites and even conducted their services in the Chinese language. They made virtually no effort to adapt themselves to Japanese culture and the needs of the common people. For this reason, they failed to exercise any influence outside of court circles. Under the favor and patronage of the court, their monasteries became wealthy and their priests powerful in politics. Eventually, their priesthood was so corrupted by good living and so active in the troubled political life of the nation that certain factions at court recognized in the Buddhist prelates a dangerous threat to their own political ambitions. When the Fujiwara family won control of the government, it moved the capital to Kyoto in order to escape the political turmoil of Nara, but the new government it established under Emperor Kwammu was eager to reform Buddhist as well as government administration. Under the patronage of the court at Kyoto, the new and different Tendai and Shingon sects flourished.

The once powerful Nara sects continued for some time to exert a cultural and political influence, but, with the development in Kyoto of Shingon and Tendai Buddhism, they lost most of their prestige. Under the impact of the great spiritual awakening of the twelfth century, they lost almost all their vitality. Three of these sects—Sanron, Jojitsu, and Kusha—died out altogether, and the Hosso, Kegon, and Ritsu sects, which still survive, continue to exist only because they have an historical interest. As the possessors of ancient and artistic temples and invaluable treasures of the Asuka and Nara periods, they have been protected by the government and are of national and even international interest. From the philosophical point of view, the doctrines of these sects are and will continue to be worth studying. But, as religions, their influence is insignificant, and they probably could not have survived to the present day without government financial support. There were in 1946 only 135,854 followers of the three remaining Nara sects.

Hosso Sect. This sect is based on a unique idealistic philosophy which teaches (1) that all empirical existences are nothing but the products of ever-changing "store-consciousness" and (2) that self-consciousness is the cause of all human delusions. It is believed that, by contemplating this "truth" in meditation and by eliminating self-consciousness, one can attain Buddhahood. The sect's head temples are Horyuji, Yakushiji, and Kofukuji. There are 77 affiliated temples and chapels, 954 priests and 57,042 adherents. It manages a college, in cooperation with the Ritsu, Kegon, and Yuzu Nembutsu sects, for the study of doctrines and the education of priests.

Kegon Sect. According to Kegon doctrines, existence for all things depends on the relationship of various causes. These interdependent existences constitute a harmonious world, a cosmos, which is conceived of as "the cosmic soul" embodied in Dainichi. Even the ego, the cause of delusions, is nothing more than a relationship of self and others. This religion aims at dispelling the illusion of a separate ego and restoring consciousness to communion with Buddha, and, through him, with other beings. The sect's great head temple is Todaiji at Nara. The sect has 126 temples, 523 priests, and 50,915 adherents. The library of the Todaiji has 30,000 books and is open to the public.

Ritsu Sect. This sect worships Buddha Dainichi. The word *ritsu*, from which the sect takes its name, originally stood for the moral precepts to be observed by priests and believers. The sect does not concern itself much with doctrinal questions but lays particular emphasis on discipline and correct succession. According to Ritsu teachings, Buddhahood can be attained only by the observance of specified moral precepts. It is believed to be the only sect in Japan in which Buddhist injunctions against the eating of meat and against marriage for the priesthood are literally observed. The grand head temple is Toshodaiji. There are 44 temples, 96 priests, and 27,897 adherents in the sect. Its library contains almost 6,000 books, including some rare and valuable documents.

Tendai Buddhism

The capital was moved to Kyoto in 794 to escape the political corruption of Nara and the ecclesiastical authorities who had

Buddhism under a monopolistic control, but this did not mean that the court had abandoned Buddhism as a religion. In an attempt to replace the less desirable aspects of Nara Buddhism with a purer spiritual religion, Emperor Kwammu sent two promising young priests to China for study. These two men, Saicho and Kukai, eventually returned to Japan and founded the Tendai and Shingon sects, which dominated the spiritual and cultural life of Japan for centuries.

Saicho (767–822), known posthumously as Dengyo Daishi, early recognized the need for religious reformation and freedom from the orthodoxy of Nara. He became a priest at the age of 13 and five years later, in 785, he founded a small hermitage on the slopes of Mount Hiei near the present city of Kyoto. This was later named Enryakuji and for eight centuries was one of the principal centers of Japanese Buddhist activity. Saicho supported the emperor and the Fujiwara family in moving the capital to Kyoto and in return received generous contributions from the government in spite of the opposition of jealous prelates in Nara. His institution on Mount Hiei grew into a large collection of sanctuaries, colleges, monasteries, and meditation halls. In 805, after returning from his studies in China, Saicho began to expound Tendai philosophy.

Tendai philosophy was eclectic. It embraced almost all of the contradictory sectarian teachings of Chinese Buddhism and it left the choice of a method of salvation largely to the individual. Its comprehensive teachings included esoteric mysteries, abstract contemplation, and faith in the saving grace of the Buddha Amida —in short, all the basic Mahayana doctrines. Saicho attempted to harmonize all beliefs and desired universal salvation. Essentially, however, Tendai emphasized the Lotus Sutra, which it considered the greatest of all Buddhist scriptures, and taught that "the supreme truth" can be realized only through meditation.

The Lotus Sutra interprets the person of Buddha as a manifestation of metaphysical entity and synthesizes the two aspects of his being: his incarnation in human life and his real ontological identity. By extension, this conception of Buddha can be applied to the relationship between individual and universal existence. The Tendai philosopher observes that the whole and all its parts are identical, that the whole cosmos is present in the minutest particle. The Tendai doctrine of ontology is an abstruse consideration of three forms of existence: the void, the temporary, and the middle. Existence or non-existence is dependent on relationship to the "middle," which is absolute existence. Tendai calls these three forms of existence the "three truths," and teaches that, when these truths are seen in perfect relationship, one has attained the enlightenment of Buddha himself. This enlightenment must be reached through philosophical training and contemplation.

The fundamental precept of Tendai ethics is to live the life of the universal self. This can be done only through initiation into a mystery which consists of making certain vows to Buddha. The doctrine of moral life, combined with faith in this mystery, is the key to perfection. Man stands midway between the height of illumination and the depths of vileness; he rises and falls according to his faith in the identity of himself with Buddha. Such faith can be achieved only through the removal of all illusion.

Tendai Buddhism reached the zenith of its influence in the ninth and tenth centuries. It materially aided the popularization of Buddhism through attempts to identify Shinto deities with those of the Buddhist pantheon, and it played an important role in educational and cultural developments. But in the eleventh and twelfth centuries a slow decline set in. Without the genius of Saicho, the differences between the conflicting doctrines he had attempted to harmonize became more pronounced, until at last, towards the end of the twelfth century, many reformers appeared within the ranks of Tendai. Unable to endure the contradictions in doctrine, these men founded independent sects which soon replaced Tendai in popularity and vigor.

Although Tendai and the monastic institutions on Mount Hiei were still financially and politically powerful, the Kamakura period saw its liturgies become formal and without substance. In the great period of political instability which continued through the sixteenth century, Tendai often resorted to force in attempting to maintain its prestige. Virtual armies of monk-soldiers occasionally descended from Mount Hiei to intimidate the decadent imperial court and burn rival religious institutions to the ground. But the new schools of Buddhism—Amida, Zen, and Nichiren—were destined to become the important centers of religion, and Tendai succumbed to their vitality.

What remained of the Tendai school was later split into many subdivisions. Various leaders created new sects within Tendai, and, during the peaceful Tokugawa Shogunate, there were signs of revival. Tendai philosophy became a favorite study of all learned priests. It even obtained considerable official support, but, with the fall of the shogunate, many estates were confiscated, and all sects of Tendai were forced to unite in 1872. The Jimon and Shinsei branches later became independent, but, again in 1941, they were forced by the government to reunite with the parent Tendai sect. In 1946, however, these became independent, as did the Shugen branch.

Tendai has survived as a religion of the upper classes, but it has some appeal for the common people as well. Some of its temples have maintained close contact with the people through social welfare work. Fees for funerals and memorial services have replaced the losses incurred by lack of aristocratic patronage.

Tendai philosophy is recognized as a brilliant spiritual achievement, and its moral idealism is still the main source of Buddhist thought in Japan. Its teachings are so comprehensive that nearly every type of doctrine may be found in them, and its ecclesiastical organization has been a model for all sects. The institutional weakness and strength of all Buddhism may be found in Tendai.

Once the greatest center of Japanese Buddhism, Tendai is still a rich field for philosophical research, but numerically it is one of the smallest branches of present-day Buddhism, its adherents numbering only slightly over 1,000,000.

Mount Hiei today is far different from what it was in 805. A little down on the eastern slope of this mountain stand a number of buildings, large and small, all half-closed and very quiet. These are known collectively as Enryakuji and stand on the site of the hermitage founded by Saicho in 785. Only the largest buildings—the Central Hall and the Assembly Hall—show signs of life, and there are few priests in attendance. Occasional services are celebrated by the priests, but very few laymen attend. The other monastic buildings are almost as silent as death, each being inhabited by only a handful of novices. Among those who picnic on the mountain, there may be groups of pilgrims, but those who visit Enryakuji are mostly curious sightseers. This is all that remains of what was the greatest center of Buddhist learning and discipline in the ninth and three succeeding centuries.

Tendai Sect. The Tendai sect, originally founded by Saicho, is one of the most distinguished in the history of Japanese Buddhism despite its present numerical inferiority to most other sects. It is the largest in the Tendai group and uses the Enryakuji as its headquarters. Followers worship the eternal Buddha S'akyamuni. The Buddhas and Bodhisattvas worshipped as incarnations of this Buddha vary according to the tradition of the temples or the training of the priests, but adherents of the Tendai sect also worship the Shinto deity Myojin, the guardian god of temples. According to the sect headquarters, the doctrine of Tendai is based on the principle that every human being is entitled to become a Buddha. Followers endeavor (1) to attain salvation for themselves and others, (2) to carry out spiritual and material improvements in human life, and (3) to promote the welfare of the nation so that the Buddhist ideal may be realized in this world.

The administration of the sect is under the control of an administrator who is concurrently the archbishop of the sect and the chief priest of the grand head temple, Enryakuji. An honorary advisory council of priests is largely under his control, and his power is only slightly limited by the sect assembly, an organization designed to handle administrative matters. Extension work is carried on by headquarters missionaries and 220 local missionaries. The sect also maintains a motion picture unit for propaganda purposes. Temples and adherents are to be found throughout the country. During the war, 167 temples belonging to this sect were totally destroyed, 11 were badly damaged, and 155 priests were killed in air raids, but the sect still has 3,708 temples, 6,880 priests, and 1,137,671 adherents.

Jimon Sect. In the year 993, almost all of the followers of Enchin (814–891), a Tendai priest, left Mount Hiei and established themselves at Mii, near Otsu, where they used a temple named Onjoji as their headquarters. Enchin was a rival of the priest Ennin, the third patriarch of Tendai. Both men were leaders in the movement to modify the teachings of Saicho by placing more emphasis on occult practices, and the split between the Tendai and Jimon sects was caused more by long standing rivalry between the followers of these two men than by disagreement over doctrines. The group which moved to Onjoji became known as the Jimon sect.

The main object of worship is the Buddha S'akyamuni, but the esoteric Buddha Dainichi is regarded as an equal to him, and other deities are worshipped as well. The Shinto deity Myojin receives homage as guardian of the temples. The traditional Tendai scriptures are used, but the *Collection of Traditional Teachings* compiled by Enchin is considered fundamental. Jimon was at one time a formidable rival to Tendai, ecclesiastically and militarily. In 1872, however, it was forced to unite with the other Tendai sects. It later became independent but, in 1941, was again forced to unite with them. Since the war, it has re-established its independence, but there is no evidence of any revival or postwar adjustments. No educational work is being carried on, and its social welfare activities are negligible. The sect today can claim only 79,290 adherents and 1,809 priests. In addition to the grand head temple, Onjoji, which is sometimes called Miidera, it has 746 temples and chapels.

Shugen Sect. En-no-Shokaku (634–701), the founder of this small esoteric sect, was the son of a Shinto priest in Yamato province near Nara. Steeped in the atmosphere of Shinto, he brought to Buddhism the ascetic practices and austerities of mountain worship. Despite his Shinto background, however, he preached that Buddha Dainichi is the central divinity of the universe. All other deities, including those of the Shinto pantheon, were considered to be revelations of his nature. The Shugen sect stresses the divine and mysterious functions of Buddha's body, speech, and mind. Mountains are believed to be manifestations of his virtue and are therefore regarded as especially holy places.

The Shugen sect is actually only one division of the school founded by En-no-Shokaku, the other division being the Daigo sect of Shingon Buddhism. En-no-Shokaku's followers maintained an independent school of Buddhism until 1872, at which time the government attempted to consolidate religious organizations.

Almost all of the members of this school allied themselves with with Shingon and called themselves the Daigo sect. However the worshippers at Shogoin, a temple very much under the influence of the Tendai sect, joined Tendai in response to the government's decrees and called themselves the Shugen Sect. This explains why Shugen, an organization whose doctrines appear to be closely related to Shingon Buddhism, is classified as a sect of Tendai Buddhism. In 1946, it regained its independence and today has 195 temples, 1,464 priests, and 29,200 adherents.

Shinsei Sect. Shinsei (1443–1495), after whom this sect is named, entered the priesthood and began studying Tendai doctrines on Mount Hiei at the age of 13. After 20 years of study, he had a vision in which the founder of Tendai gave him a treatise on Amidaism. His devotion to Amida, coupled with emphasis on Mahayana precepts, dominated his activities from then until his death. Though he made no effort to found a new sect, his followers organized themselves into a group which later became an independent sect with headquarters in a temple named Saikyoji.

Shinsei taught that the protection of the functions of body, speech, and mind was the aim of Mahayana precepts and that meditation on Buddha meant the invocation of Amida's name. The former would provide security in this world and the latter would assure rebirth in "the pure land." The most common object of worship is a statue of Amida, and the main scripture is the *Compendium on Rebirth in the Pure Land* written by the priest Genshin. Shinsei was actually an independent sect until 1872, at which time it was forced to join Tendai. In 1878, it regained its independence only to lose it again in 1941, when it was forced to rejoin Tendai. Since the war, it has declared its independence for a third time and is today the smallest of the sects traditionally associated with Tendai, having only 438 temples, 1,344 priests, and 27,618 adherents.

Shingon Buddhism

Shingon Buddhism was founded in the ninth century by Kukai (774–835), posthumously known as Kobo Daishi. He was sent to China by Emperor Kwammu, who also sent Saicho, and returned from his continental studies in 806. He selected Mount Koya, about 50 miles south of Kyoto, as the site of his monastery and for 15 years it was the center of his activities. Kukai was appointed by the Emperor as chief abbot of a great state temple in Kyoto when Saicho died. Later he became the presiding priest in the inner sanctuary of the imperial court, but, in his later years, he retired to Mount Koya, and there, according to legend, he died in 835 when he had himself buried alive in a posture of meditation.

The Shingon philosophy of Kukai was a pantheistic mysticism—a peculiar mixture of realism and idealism. According to it, the whole universe is the body of the cosmic Buddha Dainichi, and, since his body is the whole of material existence, even a grain of dust partakes of his spiritual life. As differentiated aspects of this all-embracing Buddha, Kukai's faith included a pantheon of numberless Buddhas, Bodhisattvas, deities, demons, and angels. He regarded all phenomena as activities of Buddha's body, voice, and mind. These three aspects of Buddha were termed the "three secrets," since most people are incapable of understanding them without enlightenment. However, Kukai preached that by practicing various functions of these "secrets," a person could make himself identical with Buddha in this life: by the performance of mystical signs with the fingers, by the recitation of magic formulae, and by meditation. He also believed that an esoterically adept person could invoke the power of deities and assure by this means wealth, recovery from illness, plentiful rain, good harvests, and other mundane benefits.

Kukai imported these mystic cosmological, physical, and psychological speculations almost intact from the continent, but, to Japanese Buddhism, he contributed a number of innovations of his own. He developed his own theory of the stages of spiritual development, preaching that the attainment of enlightenment must be accomplished by climbing an ascending spiritual ladder consisting of ten steps. These may be summarized as follows: (1) the mind absorbed in thoughts of food and sex, (2) recognition of moral rules and social convention, (3) innocent, childlike belief in a heavenly life, (4) awareness of the reality of existence and the nonentity of self, (5) partial enlightenment through the eradication of self-consciousness, (6) recognition of the oneness of existence and the illusory nature of external existence, (7) enlightenment as to the reality which transcends all relativities, (8) apprehension of the all-embracing "way of reality," (9) recognition of "free movement" in a world of living force, which is neither chaotic mass nor static entity, and (10) true enlightenment through comprehension of the glories of the cosmic mysteries.

Kukai's greatest innovation, however, was his unification of Buddhism and Shinto which proved to be the most important factor in the popularization of Buddhism. An attempt had been made to identify the native gods with Buddhist deities in the Nara period. Saicho also contributed much to the merging of the two religions. But it was Kukai's incarnation theory which paved the way for the ultimate amalgamation. Kukai even invented the name "Ryobu Shinto," and he is generally regarded as the founder of this dual-aspect Shinto.

In the attempt to clarify the Buddhist pantheon, a device called the *mandala* was employed on the continent. It was introduced to Japan in the Nara period and was fiirst widely used by Kukai. It became the basis for the mysterious esoteric practices and magic movements of hands and fingers which characterize Shingon Buddhism and is today employed by most Japanese Buddhist organizations. The *mandala* consists of a graphic representation of the universe in two pictures portraying "the ideal" and "the dynamic." The center of the ideal side, or "the realm of the indestructibles," is occupied by "the great illuminator" seated on a white lotus in deep contemplation, encircled by a white halo. He is surrounded by emanations in the form of figures and symbols arranged in a circular pattern of nine square frames. These represent potential ideas which will manifest themselves in the dynamic aspect of the universe. The dynamic side of cosmic life is represented by another group of deities and other beings clustered in a circular pattern around "the great illuminator." He is seated on the seed-pod of a red lotus flower which symbolizes the heart of the universe. This lotus has eight petals corresponding to the nine squares of "the indestructible cycle," and a lesser Buddha, surrounded by a double halo of red discs symbolizing activity, is seated on each petal. The surrounding groups of deities are arranged according to the kinds of powers and intentions they embody. These are divided into two classes, one representing the wisdom of the central Buddha which leads the way to universal communion and represses folly and vice, and the other representing his mercy which embraces all beings in the love of "the cosmic Buddha." The *mandala* portrays all the bodily postures and movements of hands and fingers employed in the mystic Shingon rituals and is itself an object of worship.

Through the popular appeal of esoteric practices, Shingon spread rapidly. The emphasis on the sacred functions of body, speech, and mind, the complicated manipulation of hands and fingers, the incantation of mystic formulae, and the promise of worldly profit appealed to the common people. Shingon Buddhism in the Heian period was not so much a single religious body as a mystical tendency. The very name "Shingon" is a translation of a Sanskrit term meaning "magic formula." Tendai and the classical sects of Nara were not only colored by Shingon mysticism but in many ways were completely over-shadowed by it. Shingon became very popular, entering deeply into the hearts of the people, and it left lasting traces on Japanese culture. Even the new sects of the Kamakura period did not eliminate esoteric practices. Indeed, Shingon mysticism still transcends sectarian differences and influences greatly the religious life of the Japanese people.

The history of Shingon Buddhism, however, has been varied. It offered a fruitful field for sectarian divisions and, after two centuries of great influence, the same internal corruption and secular difficulties which beset Tendai brought about its decline. Then, a reformer named Kakuban (1095–1143) did much to revive Shingon by founding a new school which came to be known as Shingi (new-teaching) Shingon. Sects which did not follow his lead are now known as Kogi (old-teaching) Shingon sects. Soon there were further sectarian divisions: Shingi Shingon became divided into the Busan and Chisan schools, and many new sects appeared within Kogi Shingon. Like Tendai, Shingon was backed by the imperial court and later by the shogunate. But vast temple estates, government support for favored temples, and other privileges which the sect had enjoyed for almost 1,000 years were either greatly reduced or completely withdrawn at the beginning of the Meiji era. Since 1900, there has been much grouping and re-grouping of sects within Shingon, and, today, there are ten major Shingon sects and a number of minor ones created only recently. In numbers of adherents, Shingon falls behind Jodo Shin and Zen, but surpasses Jodo, Nichiren, and Tendai. Unfortunately, as a school of Buddhism, Shingon lacks unity, though no doctrinal differences of any consequence divide its sects. The Shingi school is prominent chiefly in eastern Japan, while the Kogi school is prospering in western Japan.

The income of Shingon temples is derived mainly from charges for funerals, memorial services, and incantations of magic formulae for the acquisition of wealth, health, and prosperity. At some temples, the sale of talismans brings in a modest income, while some temples still cling to vast estates. There is also a small degree of support from Buddhists of other denominations since the variety of objects worshipped in Shingon ceremonies attracts members of other sects to Shingon temples.

Shingon mysticism and its practices are of interest not only to devout believers but also to students of religion. Shingon is the Japanese counterpart of Lamaism in Tibet and Mongolia, and is thus the best example of Tantric Buddhism and Hindu esotericism in Japan. The incantations and prayers of Shingon origin may not be attracting much interest for the present, but the majority of Japanese people have at least a tinge of mysticism in their spiritual heritage. Certain Shingon deities are universally popular in Japan, and this popularity will certainly not diminish appreciably in the immediate future. Mount Koya is still a great center of learning, and the influence of its university will be considerable. Major Shingon sects are making strenuous efforts to adjust their temples and institutions to the new era.

The original Shingon sect was founded by Kukai in Kyoto in 809, but, after the building of Kongobuji on Mount Koya in 818, the headquarters was moved there and the city of temples, chapels, monasteries, and cemeteries which has grown up on the summit of this mountain is still regarded as the home of Shingon Buddhism. There is today no important difference between the various sects, and it is not within the scope of this book to analyze the fine points of difference. Suffice it to say, Shingon has been one of the most alert branches of Buddhism in finding its place in the new Japan, and it can still claim approximately 9,000,000 adherents.

Amida Buddhism

The first significant development in the religious awakening of the twelfth century was the rapid spread of Amidaism. It had been included in the teachings of Saicho in the ninth century and had materially aided the popularization of Buddhism, but there was no widespread propagation of Amidaism until the twelfth century.

Amida Buddhism is believed to have originated under the influence of Hinduism in the northwestern part of India not long before the Christian era. It reached China in the second century and was brought to Japan in the sixth. Its doctrines received considerable attention in India and China and occupy perhaps a third of Mahayana literature, upon which Tendai Buddhism was founded. According to tradition, Amida was a Bodhisattva who made a solemn vow that he would not accept the supreme enlightenment of Buddhahood unless he could share his merits with all people who meditated concerning him and thereby help them to attain enlightenment. After countless ages, he accumulated a vast store of merits and attained Buddhahood, whereupon he established a western paradise, called "the pure land," in which he preaches "the law of Buddha" to the blessed. Although believers regard the Buddha Amida as an historical person, there appears to be no basis for this belief. It is likely that Amida is an abstraction whose principal attribute is infinite benevolence.

Ryonin (1072–1132), a Tendai priest, could not find in the Tendai philosophy and esotericism what he was seeking. While engaged in deep prayer and meditation in the year 1117, he had a revelation and a vision of Amida, and forthwith he traveled throughout Japan preaching Amidaism and founded the Yuzu Nembutsu sect. His philosophy, however, retained many doctrines of the older schools of thought and contained moral precepts. It was, therefore, not pure Amidaism, and it did not receive much popular support.

Amidaism came into its own with the founding of the Jodo sect in 1175 by the priest Honen (1132–1212). As a youth Honen showed great promise in his studies and, after more than 20 years of education in the Tendai institutions of Mount Hiei, had mastered the teachings of all the prominent sects of his day. But, during this period of education, he became depressed over the difficulties of attaining true enlightenment. Then, in his search for a practical and effective way of universal salvation, he came upon the following passage:

Whether walking or standing, sitting or lying, only repeat the name of Amida with all your heart. Never cease the practice of it even for a moment. This is the very work which unfailingly issues in salvation, for it is in accordance with the original vow of that Buddha.

These words made a deep impression on Honen and he founded the Jodo (Pure Land) sect on the basis of Amida's original vow. He taught that the mere recitation of the phrase "adoration to the lord of boundless light and infinite life" would give instantaneous and final assurance of rebirth in "the pure land" if it were accompanied by faith. He insisted upon the importance of repeating it as often as possible and of making this recitation the main work of life, with all other activities secondary.

The rapid spread of Honen's teaching aroused jealousy and enmity among the clergy of the established sects. On the most trivial grounds, they attempted to suppress the Jodo sect, and even the emperor took sides in the issue and banished Honen from Kyoto in 1207. But the Jodo faith had too much vitality to be suppressed by mere force. Honen was allowed to return to the capital in 1211 and found there a great popular welcome. He died the following year, and, though the hostility towards Amidaism on the part of the other sects remained unabated, Honen was succeeded by indomitable disciples who carried on his work.

Chief among the disciples of Honen was Shinran (1173–1262). He was ordained at the age of eight and began studying Mahayana Buddhism in the Tendai monasteries of Hiei. He was such an outstanding scholar that, at the age of 25, he became the head abbot of a monastery and was hailed as "the genius of Mount Hiei." But he was not in the least interested in position, fame, or power. He was seeking a way of salvation for ordinary men. At the age of 27, he heard a sermon by Honen and realized that in the teaching of Honen was the way of universal salvation which he had been seeking. He was converted to the Jodo sect in 1201 and, in his ministry and in his personal life, proved to be an extraordinary individual. He shocked the Buddhists by marrying openly. By this step, he hoped to break down the barriers between priest and layman and sought to demonstrate that true religion does not require a man to lead an abnormal life. Not only was marriage for the clergy a principle in his system, but he also ate meat and other food forbidden to the priesthood.

Shinran was exiled to Echigo when Honen and his disciples were exiled in 1207. When they were pardoned, Honen returned to Kyoto, and Shinran intended to join him there, but, when Shinran heard of Honen's death, he decided against returning to the capital immediately and took a roundabout way through outlying provinces to spread the new faith of Amidaism. It was not until 1235 that he eventually returned to Kyoto after 28 years of missionary effort.

Shinran matured and developed independently his own views

and doctrines regarding Amidaism during his separation from Honen. When he returned to the capital, Shinran discovered a doctrinal breach between himself and Honen's followers in Kyoto which could not bet bridged. Although differences in respect to doctrine are difficult to discern, Shinran founded a new sect for which he adopted the name of Jodo Shin (True Pure Land). The Jodo and Jodo Shin sect each maintains that it alone preserves the original philosophy of Honen, but the doctrinal differences are so slight that both, together with their subdivisions, are often referred to as Jodo Buddhism.

Since the thirteenth century, Amida Buddhism has been divided into many sects, yet its influence on the life and culture of the Japanese people has been tremendous. The "easy way" of Amidaism has appealed strongly to the character of the people, and it has therefore found the largest number of followers among all schools of Japanese Buddhism. It was recommended as an "easy way" because its doctrines could be understood by common people and because it required simply an expression of faith in the Buddha Amida. In contrast to the difficult doctrines and intricate practices of Tendai, Shingon, Zen, and the Nara sects, it asked little of its followers. Its doctrines of "hell" and "paradise" have become deeply rooted in the minds of devout people and are favorite themes for children's stories. Amidaism has had a real value for common people in their daily life and has provided consolation for them with its promise of life after death. Pathos, pessimism, longing after paradise, the suicide of young lovers for the sake of a happy married life in another world, the reproof to vice, and the promotion of virtue—these reflect the religious life of people imbued with the spirit of Amidaism.

The chief object of worship in the temples of this school is a statue of the Buddha Amida, and it is usually accompanied on either side by the Bodhisattva Kwannon, representing benevolence, and the Bodhisattva Daiseishi, representing wisdom. The doctrines of Amidaism are based on the "three pure land sutras," which are the *Sutra on the Buddha of Immeasurable Life,* the *Sutra on the Meditation of the Buddha of Immeasurable Life,* and the *Sutra on the Buddha Amida.* The most characteristic element of Amidaism is its use of the *nembutsu.* In the "pure land sutras" the phrase "meditation on Buddha" is written *nembutsu,* and to this meditation the idea of invocation was added. In time, meditation itself tended to become secondary or completely forgotten, so that *nembutsu* now means "calling on the name of Buddha." In Amidaism, the *nembutsu* is "adoration to the Buddha of boundless light and life"—the all-sufficient expression of faith in the ability and willingness of Amida to save, which was adopted by Honen as the foundation of his teachings. Besides the *nembutsu,* there are certain rituals and disciplines observed by priests which do not concern laymen. These are basically similar to Tendai ceremonies and disciplines; their significance, however, varies with each Amida sect.

There are four main divisions of Amidaism: Yuzu Nembutsu, Jodo, Jodo Shin, and Ji. Yuzu Nembutsu, the oldest, still shows the influence of Tendai Buddhism and does not place as much emphasis on the *nembutsu* as do the other schools. It, nevertheless, teaches that the *nembutsu* should be recited on behalf of others as well as for personal salvation. Jodo honors other Buddhas and Bodhisattvas besides Amida but teaches that salvation is best obtained by invoking the name of Amida and living a righteous life. Jodo Shin worships Amida alone. It maintains that salvation can be obtained by faith, that faith itself is the gift of Amida, and that good deeds are totally irrelevant since salvation is assured as soon as there is faith. The Ji sect also taught that salvation is experienced immediately when there is faith, and the *nembutsu* in its celebrations is often accompanied by ecstatic dancing. The Ji and Yuzu Nembutsu sects have no minor branches, but the Jodo and Jodo Shin sects are divided into numerous small branches.

Japan is undergoing great changes in every respect, and these effects of the war have not spared Amidaism. The older people, left behind by rapid and sweeping changes, still cling to their old faith and hope for rebirth in the "pure land." But the younger priests and laymen on whom the future of Amidaism depends are now thrown into confusion. Not knowing which way to turn, some have fallen into despair and are losing faith, while others are advocating radical reformation, calling for a reinterpretation of Amida and the "pure land" in conformity with modern science. Since Amidaism, with close to 22,000,000 followers, is the most powerful and active branch of Japanese Buddhism, the future of Buddhism in Japan may well depend upon the evolution of this school.

Yuzu Nembutsu Sect. This sect was founded by Ryonin (1072–1132), a Tendai priest who was one of Honen's predecessors. His doctrine is based on the Kegon teaching of the essential unity and identity of all beings and things of the universe. He taught that the merits of one man's *nembutsu* invocation are shared by the whole of existence through the principle of interpenetration, and that the merits of the *nembutsu* invocations of others are shared by "the one life" of which everyone is a part. Thus, he retained much of the philosophy of the older schools. The Yuzu Nembutsu sect used the *Sutra of a Garland of the Blossoms of Spiritual Awakening* and the *Sutra of the Lotus of the True Law* as its principal scriptures, while "the three pure land sutras" are ranked as only secondary scriptures. The object of worship in its temples is a pictorial representation of Amida surrounded by Bodhisattvas, which is said to have been the vision seen by Ryonin in 1117.

It is the only sect of Amida Buddhism which places great emphasis on moral requirements. It now has 372 temples and chapels, 346 priests, and 99,150 adherents. Upwards of 95 per cent of the believers are located in Nara and Osaka prefectures.

Jodo School. Honen Shonin, the founder of the Jodo school, is generally considered to be the father of Amida Buddhism in Japan. He began preaching Amidaism in 1175 at the age of 43 and made "the original vow" of the Buddha Amida the basis for his philosophy. His teaching had three basic principles: (1) that any common mortal may be born into the "pure land paradise," (2) that the incantation of the *nembutsu* requires neither meditation nor intellectual comprehension, but faith alone, and (3) that the efficacy of the *nembutsu* is absolute. Shortly before his death, Honen issued what is usually referred to as the "One-Sheet Document." It summarized his teachings as follows:

> The method of final salvation that I have taught is neither a sort of meditation such as that practiced by many scholars in China and Japan in the past, nor is it a repetition of the Buddha's name by those who have studied and understood the deep meaning of it. It is nothing but a mere repetition of the name of the Buddha Amida, without a doubt of his mercy, whereby one may be born into the happiest land of the Buddha.

This statement has become fundamental in the exposition of Jodo Buddhism. It was revolutionary in that it made Amida Buddhism a religion of salvation by faith alone, adding an element wholly unknown to Japanese Buddhism. The universality of this salvation naturally made Amidaism popular. As indicated previously, Amidaism met formidable opposition from the established sects, which at one time even petitioned for the prohibition of the *nembutsu*. But Jodo, with the support of the common people, continued to grow in popularity.

Jodo did not actually become an independent religious body

until early in the seventeenth century. Up to that time its numerous followers, while loyal to the Jodo teachings, technically belonged to other sects. It was the Tokugawa Shogunate that started it on a most remarkable period of independent growth and prosperity. Ieyasu, who spared neither money nor effort in order to secure divine favor from any source, believed that his successful career was due to the advice of his Jodo counsellors and therefore bestowed upon Jodo the greatest favors at his command. He contributed funds for magnificent temples and made Jodo practically the established church.

Towards the latter part of the Tokugawa period, the Jodo priests were so luxuriously provided for by their patrons that they virtually ceased all active evangelism and were content to live in ease and idleness. Hence, with the movement for restoration of imperial rule and the revival of Shinto, they became the helpless butt of their Confucian and Shinto critics. After the Meiji Restoration was accomplished, however, Jodo was quick to revitalize itself. Its leaders came to the fore in the fields of scholarship and general religious activity. The leadership of the Jodo school has been relatively progressive and constructive in matters of social welfare and relationship to the government.

The Jodo school, despite its basic doctrine of simple faith in the saving grace of Amida, includes a somewhat intricate initiation procedure for priests who rise above the status of monks. Initiation consists of five steps, or ceremonies, called the *Fivefold Transmission of Sect Teachings*. These were invented by Shogei (1341–1420) in order to create ceremonies comparable to the initiations of Shingon. By means of this procedure, priests are initiated into the deepest mysteries of the Jodo teachings. Priests are also required to observe certain precepts and take vows to realize Mahayana ideals, these having been borrowed from Tendai.

In the Jodo school, the Buddha Amida is worshipped as

81

the savior of mankind and S'akyamuni Gautama is regarded as only a revealer of Amida teachings. Many Jodo followers believe they will be greeted at death by Amida and his retinue of Bodhisattvas, headed by Kwannon and Daiseishi, who will transport them to paradise.

Jodo Buddhism is spoken of here as a school because it is actually composed of two sects: Jodo and Jodo Seizan. These sects originated through two interpretations of Honen's teachings which developed independently of the other interpretations which resulted in the Jodo Shin school of Amidaism. The differences between the Jodo and Jodo Seizan sects are slight. Of the two, the Jodo sect is by far the larger, having 7,698 temples and chapels, 18,631 priests, and 4,520,535 adherents. It teaches that, while absolute faith in the vows of Amida is essential, certain other practices are required for the attainment of Buddhahood. In addition to its many temples and chapels, it manages the Taisho University, which is also supported by Shingi Shingon and Tendai. The Jodo Seizan sect, on the other hand, lays more stress on absolute faith in Amida's "original vow." It was founded by Shoku (1177–1247), a disciple of Honen, who developed his own interpretation of Honen's "pure-land" doctrines. He preached that only faith in Amida's vow could save all beings and regarded human effort to attain salvation as ineffective. In 1919, this sect was dissolved, splitting into three minor branches. In 1941 it was again united only to redivide in 1947. Today, the three branches have 1,474 temples and chapels, 2,339 priests, and 609,679 adherents.

Ji Sect. The Ji sect was founded by Ippen (1239–1289), another Tendai priest who could not find universal salvation in Tendai doctrines. He became interested in Jodo Amidaism as interpreted by the Seizan sect, and, in 1275, in order to have confirmation of its truth, he went to Kumano Shrine, whose deity was regarded as a manifestation of Amida, and prayed for 100 days. On the last day, the deity Kumano Gongen delivered an oracle to him which confirmed his faith, so he traveled throughout the country to propagate Amidaism. The Ji sect which he founded, however, has a few doctrinal disagreements with the other sects of Amidaism. To Ippen, faith as an activity of the corrupt human mind was useless and powerless to effect salvation. He preached that the *nembutsu*, as used in his sect, is not a mere means to rebirth in "the pure land" or of the attainment of Buddhahood, but is an end in itself. Ippen said, "When I repeat the *nembutsu*, there is neither myself nor Buddha but simply the invocation." It is said that he danced in ecstasy caused by the invocation, and this ecstatic dancing while repeating the *nembutsu* became a characteristic of his sect. In modern times, however, the ecstatic dancing is usually performed by professional dancers. The Ji sect is not very large, having only 414 temples and chapels, 559 priests, and 332,100 adherents.

Jodo Shin Sect. As explained previously, Shinran, one of Honen's ablest disciples, founded the Jodo Shin (True Pure Land) sect, because, during his separation from Honen in exile, he developed interpretations of his own which differed from those of Honen's disciples in Kyoto. Both the Jodo and Jodo Shin schools maintain that they preserve the true meaning of Honen's teachings, and, though the doctrinal differences are not of any great consequence, there is sufficient disagreement to provide the basis for two schools within Jodo Buddhism.

Shinran took a roundabout route through outlying districts while returning to the capital after being pardoned and founded many temples. After roaming about through provincial towns and villages, he settled at Inada, in what is now Ibaraki prefecture, in 1217. Here he wrote his most famous work: *Teaching, Practice, Faith, and Attainment.* This was published in 1224, and the Jodo Shin sect dates its founding to the year of its publication. It was not until 1235 that Shinran returned to Kyoto, where he lived a quiet life until he died in 1263.

The fundamental teachings of the Jodo Shin sect are those of Honen as interpreted and elaborated by Shinran. Shinran accepted the "pure land" teaching of Honen but added much to it, particularly with regard to the *nembutsu*. Up to the time of Honen, the *nembutsu* practice had involved the element of meditation, and it was believed that spiritual merit was earned by its use. Honen, on the other hand, preached that the mere recitation of the *nembutsu* in simple faith would assure salvation. Shinran accepted Honen's doctrine but elaborated it with the following principles: (1) belief in the invocation of Amida's sacred name is sufficient to assure salvation, (2) in such invocation there is sufficient merit for rebirth in the "pure land," (3) when man attains this faith, his repetition of the *nembutsu* is prompted only by gratitude to Amida for salvation, and (4) the power to exercise this faith is Amida's gift and is not native to man, and, therefore, gratitude to Amida (and not sundry other religious practices) is man's chief concern. It is clear from the above that Shinran added to the doctrines of Honen the conception that faith required for salvation is itself a gift of Amida.

Rennyo (1415–1499), the eighth patriarch of Jodo Shin, is sometimes called the "second founder of the sect" because of his strenuous activities in spreading Shinran's gospel. By writing his epistles in plain language, he made his teachings understandable to the most simple-minded. Jodo Shin was primarily concerned with the life hereafter and did not lay much stress on worldly matters, but Rennyo bolstered up its weak ethical side by adding to its spiritual teachings the rule that a man saved should go through life practicing all the ordinary moralities, faithful to his duty as a citizen in the state and as a member of society and the home. Here there is a definite concern over man's duty arising from faith. Rennyo also supplied Jodo Shin with the following creed, which admirably summarizes the basic teachings of this school:

Rejecting all other religious practices and works and all idea that I can help myself, I pray wholeheartedly to Amida for my salvation in the life to come, which is the most important of all things. I believe that the moment I have faith in him my entry into the life of paradise is certain, and I exult in the thought that henceforth invocation of his name is an expression of thankfulness. Moreover, I remember with thankfulness that I have learnt this doctrine by the grace of the founder and of the righteous and wise men who succeeded him. Further, I will observe all my life the commandments as appointed.

The Jodo Shin school also teaches that, although assurance of salvation can be given in this life, enlightenment is attained in the "pure land" only after death, and that, after rebirth in the "pure land," one can voluntarily return to this world in order to engage in the work of a Buddha and help humanity in its spiritual progress. It is interesting to note that the phrase "rejecting all other religious practices and works" included in the creed automatically prevented members of the Jodo Shin school from worshipping Shinto deities as well as Buddhist deities through Ryobu Shinto. It is also important to recognize the extraordinary departures in this type of Buddhism from the original teachings of S'akyamuni, who preached that salvation can only be attained through self-enlightenment and that a person can become a Buddha in his lifetime.

The Jodo Shin school of Amida Buddhism has the greatest number of followers of all the various schools of Japanese Buddhism, but it is divided into more minor sects than any of the others. Yet the differences between these sects are not necessarily great, and the creation of independent sects was in some cases due only to geographical location. Many of them grew up around temples founded in the thirteenth century by Shinran during his missionary travels. Others are of later development, and some were even forced to become independent sects of Amidaism by government intervention. Altogether there are now approximately 16,500,000 Jodo Shin believers divided among ten sects. Two of these sects, the Honganji and Otani sects, between them claim roughly 16,000,000 followers and are the only sects of major importance.

The headquarters of both of these sects are in Kyoto, and, until the seventeenth century, they were united. When Shinran died, his daughter and grandson erected a temple in 1272 in the grounds surrounding his mausoleum at Otani in Kyoto. This became known as Honganji when it was given the title of Temple of Original Vows of Amida Who Attained Buddhahood in Time Immemorial. It was the center of Shinran's sect, but soon many internal disputes arose. In the fourteenth and fifteenth centuries, the headquarters was moved many times because of incessant civil wars and the opposition of the other schools of Buddhism. Jodo Shin had become so popular and was so envied by Tendai priests that soldier-monks from Mount Hiei eventually burned Honganji to the ground. But Jodo Shin continued to prosper. By 1580, it had become so powerful in the secular as well as the religious world that Nobunaga laid siege to the headquarters temple, which at that time was at Ishiyama. A dispute arose between the Lord Abbot and his elder son regarding the surrender of the temple, with the result that Kennyo, the Lord Abbot, bequeathed the Lord Abbotship to his second son. Upon the death of Kennyo, the question of the right of succession arose, and the followers of Honganji divided into two factions. During this dispute Ieyasu, the shogun then in power, seized this opportunity of splitting the sect, the power of which he feared, and supported the elder son, Kyonyo, by donating a tract of land on which to build a new headquarters. The Jodo Shin school was thus split into two sects. The younger son, Jungyo, used as his headquarters a tract of land in Kyoto which had been donated previously to the sect in 1591 by Hideyoshi. It became known as the Hompa Honganji sect, while the sect founded by Kyonyo, the elder son, was known as the Otani-ha Honganji sect. These are often referred to as Nishi (Western) Honganji, and Higashi (Eastern) Honganji respectively, but are officially titled the Honganji and Otani sects.

The Lord Abbots of both these sects claim direct descent from Shinran. Both have also a blood relationship to the imperial family. In 1872, the abbots of several Jodo Shin temples were raised to the peerage, and the present Lord Abbot of Honganji was given the title of a count while the present Lady Abbess of the Otani sect is a younger sister of the Empress. Both of these sects manage universities in Kyoto—the Ryukoku and the Otani Universities—and almost all the sects of Jodo Shin are widely known for their educational and social welfare activities. Of the two major sects, Otani is the larger and more influential, having 9,582 temples and chapels, 29,503 priests, and 8,484,200 adherents as compared to Honganji's 10,761 temples and chapels, 33,118 priests, and 7,378,571 adherents.

Zen Buddhism

Amidaism was the first new school of Buddhism to develop in the great spiritual awakening of the twelfth century. The second development of major significance to the religious world of Japan was the founding of Zen Buddhism. Zen teaching reached China from India in the sixth century. It was known in Japan during the Nara period and much of Zen philosophy had been included in Tendai Buddhism, but Zen did not flourish until the monk Eisai founded the Rinzai school of Zen in 1191.

Eisai (1141–1215), like the founders of the Jodo and Jodo Shin sects, was a Tendai priest who first studied Buddhism in the monasteries on Mount Hiei. Like them, he was unable to find in the voluminous scriptures of Mahayana Buddhism the "truth" he was seeking, and he traveled to China for further study. There he became interested in Zen teachings, and, after returning for a short while to Japan, he made a second trip to China during which he was converted to the Zen philosophy which had been propounded by the Indian teacher Bodhidharma in the sixth century. Upon his second return to Japan in 1191, Eisai founded the Rinzai sect in Kyoto. He obtained the favor of the reigning shogun and was later induced to move his headquarters to Kamakura. Shortly afterwards, another monk, Dogen (1200–1253), established a second school of Zen which he named the Soto sect. There is little difference between their teachings, the main distinction being that the Soto sect puts more emphasis on book learning as a supplement to meditation.

The Zen school of Buddhism, sometimes called the "school of Buddha's mind," is entirely different from any of the other schools to be found in Japan. It aims at transmitting Buddha's mind directly to the mind of believers. Silent meditation and abstract contemplation are its chief characteristics. It holds that enlightenment can come only by intuitive thought. Sacred formulae, faith in a savior, and personal effort to understand the meaning of the universe have no place in Zen. What is required is an immediate aesthetic perception of reality. Since it is an intuitive method of spiritual training, it cannot be formulated into tenets or follow the usual channels of reasoning. There is, therefore, no dependence on scriptures, sacred writing, or sermons. The "truth" of Zen must be transmitted through spiritual telepathy, and it is said the students often practice its mental disciplines for many years before attaining enlightenment in a sudden, overwhelming revelation of the true nature of the universe.

Zen teachings include recommendations regarding proper postures for meditation and elaborate rules for the disciplining of the mind, but these are only designed to facilitate a kind of mystical self-intoxication through which one may escape consciousness of the self and all individual existence and enter into a feeling of oneness with reality. According to Zen, there is a fundamental unity in existence which underlies all experience and all phenomena. Man attains enlightenment when, through meditation in which his mind becomes a holy vacancy, he absorbs the universe into himself. Only then can he transcend the vicissitudes of life, detach himself from concern for personal gain or pleasure, and remain undisturbed in the face of calamities and adversity. Bodhidharma, the Indian who brought Zen from India to China in the year 520, once sat silently staring at a blank wall for nine years during which time he refused to answer questions concerning himself or his religion. This kind of mental discipline and self-intoxication are characteristic of Zen. The requirements of this school are often summarized in the following quotation:

Special transmission outside the scriptures; no dependence upon words and letters; direct pointing to the soul of man; seeing into one's nature; and the attainment of Buddhahood.

The Zen school claims that it most accurately represents the philosophy of S'akyamuni. This claim appears to be substantiated since Zen emphasizes meditation and self-discipline more than the other schools, but Zen philosophy, in addition to the practice of meditation and mystical communion with the universe, includes a considerable emphasis on Chinese aestheticism.

Zen monks introduced from China the teachings of Shushi, a Chinese Confucian philosopher of the twelfth century, which, in the seventeenth century, became the foundation of *bushido*, "the way of the warrior." In Zen educational institutions, there was increasing stress laid on Confucian doctrines, and, while the religious life of the people was dominated by Buddhism, the practical ethics of the nation and the feudal government system were dominated by Confucian thought. It was this Shushi school of Confucianism, fostered by Zen, which promoted an alliance with Shinto and ultimately led to the Shinto renaissance and its disastrous aftermath.

In the seventeenth century, a new branch of Zen called the Obaku sect was introduced from China. But, despite its association with the military and the influence of its priests in educational circles, Zen power began to wane in the Tokugawa period, and Zen lost much of its prestige. Because of its close connection with Confucianism and *bushido*, however, it has always had a strong, indirect influence on the thought and conduct of both the official class and the common people. No other form of Buddhism has had such a lasting influence on the life and culture of the nation. Its spirit has become the essence of the finest Japanese culture. Zen contributed much to the architecture, literature, painting, manners, dramas, and dancing of Japan. The celebrated Noh plays and the popular tea ceremony were introduced by Zen. Aesthetic enjoyment of a highly refined nature is characteristic of all Zen devotees, and the type of conduct usually expressed by the words "Japanese spirit" is essentially Zen in nature.

Today Zen has nearly 9,000,000 followers and is a powerful force in Japanese religious life. Not being bound to ancient scriptures, mystical formulae, or asceticism, and being almost wholly devoid of the superstitious practices so characteristic of Buddhism in general, Zen offers in its emphasis on meditation and self-improvement either a means for the Japanese to preserve the basic values in their ancient traditions and thus to tide over the tremendous reforms and innovations sweeping the country, or an open road for a spontaneous evolution of Japanese culture and religion in keeping with the progressive elements in world culture and philosophy.

Rinzai School. Rinzai is really more of a school than a sect. It consists of 15 orders most of which were established in the thirteenth and fourteenth centuries, the first order having been founded by Eisai in 1191. Only a loose administrative organization for conference and cooperative effort links these together. Each order has its own chief abbot and sect organization. Most of the headquarters and large temples are located in the vicinity of Kyoto, and the largest and most influential of these orders is Myoshinji, to which 60 per cent of Rinzai temples and 66 per cent of Rinzai adherents belong.

The chief difference between Rinzai and Soto doctrines is that Rinzai attaches less importance to book learning. Yet, in addition to certain texts common to all Zen sects, it has several treatises which it utilizes as subjects for meditation; in Rinzai monasteries, it is customary for the chief abbot to give priests themes for meditation. There are few doctrinal differences between the sects of this school, and combined they have 6,007 temples, 10,747 priests, and 2,328,370 adherents.

Soto Sect. The Soto sect, founded by Dogen shortly after Eisai founded the Rinzai school, is the most active and influential branch of Zen Buddhism. It carries on widespread propaganda activities and sends missionaries throughout the country. It maintains a university and several middle schools. It is constantly engaged in social welfare work. Its followers can be found everywhere in Japan. Its teachings differ from those of Rinzai in that it emphasizes the gradual development of enlightenment and employs book learning as an aid to silent meditation. Its rules for meditative postures and practices are not as strict as those of Rinzai, and its teachings place more emphasis on morality and good conduct. The headquarters of this sect is in Tokyo and it owns 14,895 temples, has 31,084 priests, and claims 6,408,622 adherents.

Obaku Sect. Obaku is a small sect which falls under the category of Zen Buddhism but which, in its teachings and practices, has elements foreign to the other schools of Zen. Obaku was founded by a Chinese priest named Ingen (1592–1673) and has the appearance of a Chinese transplantation since it conducts its ceremonies and services according to the style of the Ming dynasty. It is unique among the Zen sects also in that it uses the works of its founder, Ingen, as scriptures and includes the Amida Sutra in its doctrinal system. It stresses the immanence of the Buddha Amida in the human mind. It is a scholarly sect and has contributed much in the way of research in Chinese classics. It has 516 temples, 837 priests, and 117,224 adherents.

Nichiren Buddhism

The twelfth century witnessed a great revival of interest in religion with the birth of Amidaism and Zen Buddhism. Towards the middle of the thirteenth century, there was a third major development in this remarkable period in Japan's religious history when a great reformer named Nichiren appeared on the scene. Nichiren (1222–1282) was a dynamic figure, a fiery man of action, and stands out as one of the greatest figures in Japanese history. At 15, he was ordained a monk and, at 20, was studying on Mount Hiei. Like the founders of the Zen and Amida schools, he learned his Buddhism through Tendai doctrines. But, in his studies, he perceived that Buddhism had been divided and weakened by sectarian differences and secular interests. He regarded all the sectarian interpretations of his day as nothing more than perversions of S'akyamuni's teachings and earnestly desired to restore Buddhism to the pure religion of its founder.

While studying on Mount Hiei, Nichiren became absorbed in the teachings of the Lotus Sutra, and it later became the principal scripture of his sect. The Lotus Sutra was written some centuries after the time of S'akyamuni. Interpreters of the Lotus Sutra usually divided it into two parts of fourteen chapters each, calling the first part the "shadow gate" and the second part the "true gate." The "shadow gate" portion deals with S'akyamuni and the "law" he taught; the "true gate" portion reveals S'akyamuni as the "eternal Buddha of original enlightenment" and describes how he called out of the earth his primordial disciple Jogyo Bosatsu and entrusted to him the salvation of all beings in the "age of the latter law." It is interesting to note that, although Nichiren wished to return to the religion of S'akyamuni, he unfortunately did not know what pure Buddhism was and selected this sutra as the basis for his faith. There is no substantial evidence that S'akyamuni ever mentioned an "eternal Buddha of original enlightenment" in his teaching. He certainly did not identify himself with any such entity.

Ten years after taking up his studies in the Tendai institutions, Nichiren returned to his home in Awa province. Early one summer morning in the year 1253 he climbed to the summit of a near-by hill and proclaimed, "Hail, thou scripture of the lotus of the true law!" Nichiren's followers date the origin of their sect from this date. Nichiren, however, did not intend to found a new sect. He merely wished to reform Buddhism and restore to it what he believed to be the original meaning of S'akyamuni's teachings. He, therefore, began by denouncing what he considered the intellectual degeneracy of the current sects. No school of Buddhism escaped the force of his criticism, but he centered his attack on Amidaism, because he felt it was depriving S'akyamuni of his true glory and giving it to Amida. Its promise of rebirth in the pure land, or western paradise, he found particularly obnoxious.

Propagation of his new faith and his bitter attacks on other religious bodies quite naturally resulted in much persecution. Nichiren was driven out of his native province, and he selected Kamakura, the seat of the shogunate government, as a new field for his activities. Here he resumed his tirades against the corrupt religion of his day and began also to denounce the state of the nation. He considered participation in secular affairs by the church and political separation between the court and military governments as indications of national disunity. And he prophesied that, if Japan remained a divided nation, both religion and the state would be destroyed. Nor did Nichiren prove to be a mere alarmist, for, shortly afterwards, Japan barely managed, with the aid of natural elements, to repel an invasion of Mongols from China, and famine and disease in the wake of severe earthquakes and hurricanes devastated the country. Nichiren ascribed all of these calamities to corrupt religion and promised more disasters if the nation did not turn to his pure faith.

Nichiren's continued attacks on the currently popular Amidaism and his criticism of the government led to severe reprisals. He was accused of heresy and of inciting rebellion and was banished in 1261. He returned to Kamakura three years later and continued his tirades with renewed vigor. Again he was banished, this time barely escaping martyrdom when a death sentence passed on him by the court was commuted to exile. These persecutions only served to increase his ardor, however, and, by 1272, he had gained so much support that he was able to return to Kamakura to carry on his work. During his trials and persecutions, Nichiren came to believe he was the reincarnation of Bosatsu Jogyo, the disciple of S'akyamuni mentioned in the Lotus Sutra. His fanaticism was extreme, and he regarded himself as the savior of the nation in a time of crisis. In 1274, however, Nichiren suddenly retired to Mount Minobu, near Mount Fuji. He died in 1282 at Ikegami, near Tokyo, while journeying to some hot springs.

In spite of early opposition, Nichiren's followers organized themselves into an active sect which gained the interest of the court nobles, and, in 1321, they received imperial authority to build a temple in Kyoto. But the opposition was not easily silenced; Jodo and Tendai were both jeolous of the Nichirenites. In the course of the next few centuries, many disputes and armed clashes occurred. In 1536, armed monks descended from Mount Hiei and burned the Nichiren temples in Kyoto. The combination of religious fervor and political agitation found in Nichirenism appealed to the militant spirit of the unsettled fourteenth, fifteenth, and sixteenth centuries, but, when the Tokugawas got into power, they would no longer tolerate its disrupting influence. Nichirenism, however, continued to grow in influence among the bourgeoisie and lower classes. With the development of Japan during the Meiji period, many factors caused it to become a strong influence in the expanding empire. The romantic and daring prophet became an object of hero worship for the patriotic, his intellectualism inspired the intelligentsia, and his religious ardor aroused the devotion of the religious. Fanatical nationalists are often linked with the name of Nichiren, although Nichiren was not more than patriotic. In view of the fanaticism of its adherents, Nichiren represents today a vital force in Japanese Buddhism, although it falls far behind the Amida, Zen, and Shingon sects in numbers of adherents.

Nichiren Buddhism is a development from elements present

in Tendai doctrines, but, in contrast to Tendai, its doctrines are narrow and exclusive. In Tendai, the Lotus Sutra is only one of the scriptures; in Nichirenism, it is the only scripture. The virulent attacks on other sects by Nichirenites grew out of this conviction. And, within the ranks of Nichiren's followers, many of the sectarian controversies have raged over interpretation of this sutra, some sects claiming the superiority of the "true gate" portion while others maintain that both parts are essentially identical. In addition to the Lotus Sutra, there are the "three great secret laws," namely the "great *mandala*," the "sacred formula," and the "precept platform." The main object of worship is the "great *mandala*," in which the eternal Buddha and his manifestations in the idealistic world are graphically represented. A Nichiren Buddhist believes that when he repeats the sacred formula "Adoration to the sutra of the lotus of the true law" his soul becomes identified with the cosmic soul of the eternal Buddha. The sacred formula is, therefore, the means of salvation; it alone is sufficient. But this does not preclude the desirability of memorizing long passages from the sutra, and some of the sects are famous for this. The "precept platform" was originally a place of ordination, but in the Nichirenism of today it means the holy center of the ecclesiastical order for Japan and for the world. Some Nichiren followers hope to make their temple at Mount Minobu, near the foot of Mount Fuji, the religious capital of the world.

Stated simply, Nichiren Buddhism teaches that anyone who utters the sacred formula attains Buddhahood, receives the moral virtue comprised in the formula, and becomes in himself an embodiment of paradise on this earth. Due to conflicting interpretations of Nichiren's teachings, however, the Nichiren school of Buddhism has split into many sects. Some of these are small and of very recent origin. The Showa Hon sect, for instance, was founded as recently as 1946 and has only 50 adherents, who chant the sacred formula incessantly, believing that all other sects of Nichirenism are corrupt and that chanting the sacred formula will bring about the salvation of the world. The sect has no temple, and the founder prohibits the possession of private property and the collection of fees. That is one extreme of Nichirenism. On the other hand, there are many large sects with hundreds of thousands of adherents and many temples and priests. There are altogether about 2,000,000 Nichirenites, divided into many sects.

6

SHINTO: NATURE AND TYPES

Shinto, to many non-Japanese, means simply a *torii*, a shrine, or an ultranationalistic religion which made the Japanese people a nation of emperor-worshipping chauvinists. It is sometimes erroneously supposed that the Occupation abolished Shinto. State Shinto, a religious system fostered and supported by the government, was banned and every effort made to enforce the directives issued regarding the dissolution of this supra-religious cult. But Shinto itself is something much broader than State Shinto and, as a religion, remained at liberty to maintain and propagate its faith and practices.

Shinto, "the way of the gods," has no official scriptures, no founder, and no organized teachings; yet it is a powerful religious influence. A composite of man's multifarious responses to his natural and human environment, it is a way of life inextricably woven into the texture of Japanese thought and conduct. Some of its ideology proved to be a menace to the world. But there is much in it that is simple, naive, and politically innocuous. A considerable body of its doctrines would seem to have value in continually enriching the life of the people in the achievement of a higher culture.

Shinto is the indigenous religion of Japan. From time immemorial it has been a part of the Japanese way of life and has been subjected to so many foreign influences that definition is not easy. As a religion it is concerned with a variety of deities, known as *kami*, which vary in nature from the spirits of trees, foxes, and mountains to deified ancestors, heroes, emperors, and a pantheon of heavenly deities, chief among whom is the Sun Goddess. The worship of these *kami* centers in the observance of ceremonies and festivals which are closely related to community and national traditions. There are at present many types of Shinto, and no purpose would be served by a discussion of a correct definition of the religion. The fundamental nature of Shinto rather than academic definition is the real point of interest. In order to understand the basic nature of this religion, one must begin with an examination of primitive Shinto, for, with few exceptions, the modern forms of Shinto are rooted in the indigenous faith of ancient Japan.

Primitive Shinto

Religion in ancient Japan was a combination of animism and nature worship. All things animate or inanimate—people, objects, and natural phenomena—were believed to have souls or spirits and were apparently thought to possess the power of speech. This soul was the spiritual essence, that which gives life or activity to substance, even inanimate substance. Deities were called *kami*, and this term was applied to the deities of heaven and earth, to their spirits which dwelt in shrines, and to beasts, birds, plants, seas, mountains, and to such natural phenomena as storms, winds, and echoes. Apparently, the early Japanese worshipped the divine spirit in anything, whether noble or malignant, which seemed to possess extraordinary powers or qualities which evoked awe.

Kami is a word with such a variety of meanings that no truly accurate definition of it can be given. The literal translation of the character by which it is represented is "above," and it is generally used to imply superiority. When used to imply spiritual superiority, it may be permissible to translate it as "god," but it should be realized that, when used in this connection, it means to the Japanese an object of reverence rather than of worship in the Occidental sense. It is still a common word used to indicate, among other things, mere superiority of location or rank. The early Japanese applied it indiscriminately to any object, animate or inanimate, which was superior, mysterious, fearful, powerful, or incomprehensible. One must grasp this simple concept of deity if he is to understand the basic meaning of *kami*.

Man's approach to the *kami* was one of friendly intimacy. He felt love and gratitude and the desire to console or placate. Fear was almost totally absent. The idea of the soul and the distinctions between life and death—body and spirit—were extremely vague, however, and this early religion appears to have lacked speculative philosophical elements. There was little differentiation between worship of an object as a deity, worship of its spirit, and worship of its attributes. Life and growth were desirable; decay and death were evils to be avoided. Anthropomorphism was common but undeveloped.

There was hardly any ancestor worship in ancient Japan, and the bodies of the dead were treated with no special respect. One common method for disposing of bodies was to expose them in trees. Later, burial in mounds or tombs was adopted. If there was ancestor worship, it was probably known only to the ruling family and the upper class. There are some students of history who claim that certain *kami* were personified objects or phenomena which later came to be regarded as ancestors, and others who claim that they were actually ancestors who became posthumously identified with deified objects or phenomena. Some

100

even claim, for instance, that the Sun Goddess was actually an ancestress who was deified and identified with the sun. It is certain, however, that, until the introduction of Chinese civilization, ancestor worship was extremely vague and unsystematized.

Since the early Japanese lived in an agricultural society, interest in fertility and food production was dominant. Prominent among the deities worshipped were the goddess of food, the god of grains, and other deities, such as the storm god, who directly affected the welfare of the people through their connection with food production. The personification of the sun was in part an expression of this interest. Phallicism, one phase of the idea of fertility, was very prevalent. And the most important festivals were those related to harvests.

The one essential for approaching the deities was purification. Disease, wounds, death, sexual intercourse, and menstruation were regarded as defilements. Before participating in any Shinto ritual, the worshipper would not only cleanse himself physically but would also seek to purify such pollutions. There was no sense of moral guilt or sin in Shinto. All that was required was ceremonial purification in the presence of the deities. This purification was accomplished by various magical rites, which still provide the basis for the many purification rituals to be found in modern Shinto.

The worshipper in prehistoric antiquity usually faced the object of devotion itself, which might be a tree, stone, mountain, or sunrise. He performed his devotions standing within a sacred enclosure, which was often set within a quiet grove. In time, a shrine was erected at the spot, or, if the object of worship was a distant mountain, only a covering was prepared under which the worshipper might stand. The shrines were always of extremely simple construction with no decorative effects, usually nothing more than a thatched roof supported by straight pillars. Within there would be a symbolic representation of deity, a substitute spirit which might be a stone, a mirror, or some other symbol of divinity. There were no images in ancient Shinto. Around the precincts could be found straw ropes from which were suspended small strips of paper. These marked off the sacred spot and were to protect the objects of worship from evil influences. And inside the shrines there were small wands or short sticks with hemp or paper strips inserted at one end. These were symbolic offerings and occasionally were regarded as symbols of divinity. At the entrance to the shrine compound, there stood a *torii*, a symbolic gateway dividing the sacred from the secular. Somewhere near the shrine, there would be fresh water, a spring or a basin, for the purification of the worshippers.

Along with simple nature and spirit worship, there was the worship of clan deities. These tutelary deities were those which were believed to be the particular benefactors of each community or which in some cases were thought to be the progenitors of the clans. The common beliefs and traditions of the clans were based on these clan cults. The family head was both father and chief priest. In time, there developed the practice of revering ancestral or tutelary deities. The ascendancy of the Yamato clan raised its clan deity, the Sun Goddess, to the position of ancestress of all other clans. While she achieved this position of grandeur and her qualities became more clearly defined, she also became more remote, and local deities took on a deeper meaning by sharing in her reflected glory.

Early Mythology

On the one hand, there had developed a religious system devoted to nature deities of more or less local interest; on the other hand, there had come into being a national cult centering in the Sun Goddess, who was regarded as the guardian of agriculture and the ancestress of the ruling family. Due to the lack of historical texts prior to the seventh and eighth centuries, it is almost impossible to tell the exact nature of the Sun Goddess cult before it was subjected to foreign influences. Without doubt, the compilers of the first historical narratives colored their accounts and, in some cases, added ideas and traditions not indigenous to Japan. The *Kojiki* (Chronicle of Ancient Events) and the *Nihongi* (Chronicles of Japan) were the first scriptures of Shinto, and the religious ideas they present have persisted to modern times. The cycle of cosmological myths centering in three creative deities, who are said to have come from primeval chaos, are Chinese in origin and played very little part in Shinto festivals. The trinity consists of a central deity, the Heavenly-Central-Lord (Ame-no-minakanushi) and two subordinates, the High-Producing (Takami-musubi) and the Divine-Producing (Kami-musubi), who appear to represent the male and female principles. These three deities of creation gradually disappeared in Shinto worship, as did a succession of similar deities, but they reappeared in the Tokugawa period and are indicative of a monotheistic or at least henotheistic tendency in Shinto.

The last of the succession of deities mentioned above were the Male-Who-Invites (Izanagi) and the Female-Who-Invites (Izanami). These produced the terrestrial world and gave birth to wind, water, mists, food, mountains, and other natural phenomena which also became deities. The ideas of spontaneous and sexual generation exist side by side in Japanese mythology with complete naivete. The final offspring of this divine couple were the Heavenly-Shining-Goddess (Amaterasu Omikami), the Moon-Ruler (Tsuki-yomi), and the Valiant-Swift-Impetuous-Hero (Take-haya-susanowo). The Sun Goddess ruled the realm of light, including heaven and earth; the Moon God ruled the night; and

103

the Valiant-Swift-Impetuous-Hero ruled the mysterious nether regions.

The Sun Goddess became the progenitrix of a line of lesser deities who, according to the official myth, ruled the world. As the ancestress of Emperor Jimmu, ruler of the conquering Yamato clan, she dominated all other clan deities and came to be worshipped as the progenitrix of the entire race. The three insignia of the imperial throne—a mirror, a sword, and a jewel—were legendary gifts from her to the Yamato rulers. As the supreme deity of Shinto, her worship has occasionally given impetus to monotheistic trends in Shinto.

Foreign Influences

This, in brief, was primitive Shinto before the impact of Chinese civilization was fully felt. To a surprising degree, the same basic ideas, ceremonies, and mythology prevail today. But, through the centuries, Shinto was subjected to various influences from abroad, the effects of which cannot be ignored. The introduction of Chinese civilization brought about remarkable transformation in the life of the Japanese people, and, although the indigenous beliefs showed great tenacity, Shinto gradually absorbed elements of Taoism, Confucianism, dualism, and Buddhism. Indeed, from the ninth to the nineteenth century, Shinto was so overshadowed by Buddhism and absorbed so completely into the Buddhist system that it was engaged in a constant struggle for survival.

The greatest influence of all was exerted by Buddhism. It was even Buddhism which caused the adoption of the term "Shinto." Confronted with serious competition from Buddhist priests, Shinto priests adopted the practice of astrology, geomancy, and magic to regain prestige, and many Shinto cults came into being which developed doctrinal foundations and later became the nuclei of Shinto sects. Through dual-aspect Shinto and the adaptation of the Buddhist incarnation theory to include Shinto deities, Buddhism brought about the inclusion of foreign gods in the Shinto pantheon, and Shinto lost most of its unique character. The form of Shinto rituals and even the design of Shinto shrines was very much influenced by Buddhism. Visual objects for deities were introduced so that wooden statues and religious pictures were placed within the shrines. The traditional simplicity of the shrines was abandoned and ornate styles with brilliant coloring were adopted. Thus, while shrine and temple architecture are very distinct in their pure form and would never be mistaken, there are now a great many sanctuaries in Japan which could easily be either Shinto shrines or Buddhist temples. Many of these innovations resulting from the fusion with Buddhism were swept away in the triumph of renascent Shinto in the nineteenth century, but the most important contribution of Buddhism is still retained by Shinto. This was the deepening and broadening of the ethical content of the primitive religion and the widening of its philosophical outlook.

Taoist influence has penetrated rather deeply into Shinto, although there has never been any kind of Taoist organization in Japan. Animistic beliefs, with their accompanying magic and sorcery, appear to have been influenced by Taoism. Ascetic practices characteristic of certain Shinto sects are suggestive of Taoism, and it is apparent that the leaders of renascent Shinto were students of Taoism. It is not clear whether the shamanism of Japan is indigenous or a product of Taoist influence.

Chinese dualism is another element which modified Shinto. Its influence antedates that of Buddhism, and the two principles of *yin* and *yang* and the theory of the five elements—wood, earth, fire, metal, and water—were known in Japan as early as the fourth century. Their effect on divination, fortunetelling, and augury was far-reaching. The Japanese called the practices associated with these dualistic astrological ideas *Onyo-do,* and the guidance of private lives and even government policies on the strength of these cosmological principles became an integral part of Shinto practice.

The contribution of Confucianism to Shinto during the course of the centuries was very great. It did not at first exert much influence on the everyday religion of the common people, but the continental superstitions it carried with it, including dualism, soon found their way into the religious practices of the whole nation. It stimulated Japanese ancestor worship and spread it to all classes of people. Confucianism's greatest contribution was a satisfactory system of ethics which became the guide for Japanese social conduct and the basis of feudal society. It provided the Japanese with a new theory of study based on Confucian practical politics, and it was the study of Confucianism in the eighteenth and nineteenth centuries which caused students of history to reflect on the situation in Japan and gave rise to the loyalist movement which culminated in the restoration of imperial rule. Members of the Shushi and Mito schools of Confucianism were appalled at the degeneracy of the nation, with its emperor under the power of a military dictator and with its native religion corrupted by the encroachments of Buddhism. The interest in ancient Japanese traditions aroused by these Confucian scholars burst forth in the loyalist movement, which swept the shogunate out of power, re-established the rule of the emperor, and made Shinto the national cult, transcending all religions.

Types of Shinto

After the Meiji Restoration, Shinto was divided into two

main groups, State and Sectarian, but this classification is only superficially satisfactory. The division is artifical and was made for the convenience of the government. And, in addition to State and Sectarian Shinto, there was what might be called Popular Shinto which, though unorganized into sects, encompassed the entire field of Shinto.

State Shinto was the national cult officially sponsored by the government for the purpose of inculcating loyalty and obedience. It was officially declared to be non-religious, and, in practice, this meant that it transcended religion. Included in State Shinto were Tennoism, Imperial Family Shinto, Household Shinto, and Shrine Shinto. The government fostered these branches of the Shinto religion through official acts, financial support, instruction in public schools, and propaganda. It was against State Shinto that the Occupation directives were primarily aimed. These so altered the Shinto religious organizations that State Shinto, as such, ceased to exist. Imperial Family Shinto, Household Shinto, and Shrine Shinto continued to exist, but they were now without government support and must be considered in the same light as Sectarian Shinto and Popular Shinto.

Sectarian Shinto consists mainly of 13 sects which were permitted by the Meiji government to organize themselves into religious bodies with independent administrative organizations. Some are based on ancient Shinto practices, some are based on doctrines which, though founded on Shinto, appeared for the first time in the modern era, and some are not Shinto at all. These sects were classified as Shinto by the government for lack of a better description. In the postwar period a number of new religious bodies have grown up within the ranks of these sects, and, taking advantage of the new religious freedom, they have declared their independence. They are still nebulous, and not much is definitely known about them, so, for the present purposes, they will be discussed in the chapter on New Sects.

Popular Shinto includes an unnumbered variety of curious deities who are held in various degrees of respect, a large number of cults which heretofore have been suppressed by the government, and a body of superstitious or magical beliefs and practices which show strong Shinto influence.

The following discussion of the various types of Shinto includes Tennoism, Imperial Family Shinto, Household Shinto, and Popular Beliefs. Shrine Shinto and Sectarian Shinto, however, because of their greater importance, will be treated at greater length in separate chapters.

Tennoism

Tennoism, or Kokutai Shinto, is belief in the emperor (*tenno*) as the living incarnation of the Sun Goddess, and thus as a manifestation of the Absolute. Emperor worship is one of the oldest traditions of the Japanese people and dates back to the first centuries of the Christian era when the Yamato clan first gained ascendancy over the nation. Being not only the ruler but also the chief priest of the nation, the emperor became the chief intermediary between the people and the Sun Goddess. According to legends and mythology, he was the direct descendant of the deities who created Japan and the universe, and the cult of emperor worship, strengthened by Confucian doctrines of loyalty for ancestors, spread throughout the entire nation.

During the turbulent "dark ages" of Japan's history, there was little concern for emperor worship, and the imperial family, helpless in the power of military dictators, lived in obscurity and often extreme poverty. The course of events leading up to the Meiji Restoration revived the interest of the people in Shinto and imperial rule, and the emperor became the rallying point of the forces which sought to overthrow the Tokugawa Shogunate. When the Restoration was accomplished, the emperor again became the head of the nation. Although there was little basis in fact for the idea that the emperor had always ruled the nation, the first article of the new constitution proclaimed that the imperial family had ruled Japan for ages eternal, and the third article declared that the emperor was sacred and inviolable. The founders of the new Japan were content to manufacture history, and they moulded the minds of the people to their own ends. Their aim was the establishment of a family-state based on worship of the Sun Goddess, the extreme development of a chauvinistic renascent Shinto. The word used to described this idea was *kokutai*, which may be freely translated "national structure." Worship of the emperor was the cardinal principle of this new "national structure," and the Imperial Rescript on Education issued in 1890 was considered a sacred text setting forth the morality for emperor worship.

The position taken by exponents of emperor worship was often extreme. The sovereign was described as partaking of divine virtue, as being the symbol of the infallibility of imperial authority. He was regarded as a virtual god in human shape, and the loyalty of his subjects was similar to a religious devotion. The entire nation was believed by some to be specially favored by the gods.

In its most extreme sense, emperor worship led to the popular belief that the head of the Japanese nation was by divine authority the ruler of the universe. This view was officially sponsored through government propaganda agencies and led to firm conviction on the part of some of the Japanese that their nation was destined to rule the world. In varying degrees, this point of view entered into the teachings of not only those who were devotees of State Shinto but of all schools of Shinto, and to some extent the entire nation, including other religious bodies.

Imperial Family Shinto

The imperial family ceremonies concern the nation as a whole only indirectly, so they need not be discussed in detail. There are four shrines within the palace grounds devoted to the exclusive use of the imperial family. Those are the Kashiko-dokoro, dedicated to Amaterasu Omikami; the Korei-den, dedicated to the emperors of the past; the Shin-den, dedicated to the eight myriads of gods; and the Shinka-den, which has no special object of worship. The first three shrines are located in one building and all festivals except the Harvest Festival (*Niiname-sai*) are celebrated there. The Kashiko-dokoro, which is a branch shrine of the Grand Shrine of Ise, is the central one of the three. At the Harvest Festival the presence of the Sun Goddess is invoked at the Shinka-den, and thanksgiving is offered to her there. Nearly all of the ceremonies observed at these shrines are unique. They concern the imperial family traditions and are the private affair of the emperor, who is free to worship as he wishes.

Household Shinto

Household Shinto ceremonies are, as would be expected, concerned with family matters, particularly anniversaries of the death of relatives and ancestors. A miniature shrine, which can be purchased in the shopping district of any town, is usually placed in the living room in a small alcove above a closet door. Within it are sacred tablets, one from the Grand Shrine of Ise and one from the tutelary shrine. This small shrine, which is usually referred to as a god-shelf (*kamidana*), serves as a family altar. Immediately in front of the god-shelf, there is a tiny stand for an offering, and, at either side, there may be candles. A hemp rope with paper strips attached to it hangs above the family shrine, and there may be memorial tablets for deceased relatives hanging just below and perhaps to one side of the altar.

The earnest Shintoist will rise in the morning, perform his ablutions, and then step in front of the shrine. There he will bow, clap his hands twice, bow for a moment in silence, and then depart, ready for the day's activities. On special occasions, he will purify himself by bathing, and, sometimes, he will add a cold plunge by way of simple austerity. Then, as he stands before the shrine, he will purify himself by waving before him over each shoulder either a small branch of the sacred *sakaki* tree or an imitation made of hemp and paper cuttings attached to a wand. If the home has a small shrine in the garden, these observances will take place there. The worshipper will step into the garden, face the rising sun, a mountain, Ise, or some similarly sacred place, clap his hands, and then bow for a moment in silence. In inclement weather this ceremony is naturally performed within the house.

Special occasions, such as the naming of a child on the seventh day after birth and the visits to the tutelary shrine on the thirty-first and thirty-third day after birth, will be announced at the family altar before proceeding to the tutelary shrine. If the home can afford it, a priest is often called in to commemorate the anniversary of the death of some relative or ancestor. A photograph of the person in question will be put before the shrine. Ritual prayers are chanted as part of the service, and recollections of the departed will be exchanged and a feast enjoyed. If no priest is called in, the head of the family performs the rites and chants the prayers if he knows them.

Since household worship depends entirely on the earnestness of the parents, the effect of this domestic worship is incalculable.

The government naturally did everything possible to foster family worship. Prior to and during the recent conflict, great stress was laid on having a shrine in every home, and, in the eyes of the state, true patriotism involved the worship of Shinto deities through Household Shinto. However, the strongest Buddhist sect, Jodo Shin, and many Christians apparently held out against having such shrines in their homes, although in other ways they paid lip service to the Shinto gods of the nation.

Popular Beliefs

There are numerous Shinto beliefs and practices not generally included in either Shrine Shinto or Sectarian Shinto, and it is these aspects of Shinto which are referred to by the term "popular beliefs." These beliefs and practices include the popular deities whose images dot the countryside, superstitions, and occult practices regarding such things as divination, spirit possession, and magical protection from disease. Any one or even several of these factors may be found in the recognized sects, shrines, or temples, but they are more commonly found in the vast, unorganized field of popular beliefs and practices.

Among the innumerable images to be found throughout the length and breadth of the land, the most common are essentially of Shinto origin, even though some may show very strong continental influence. Prominent among such deities are: Doso-jin, the guardian of the crossroads; Kamado-no-kami, who presides over the kitchen fires; Ryu-jin, a serpent deity who acts as a guardian god and is also believed to control the wind and the rain; and Daikokuten, one of the seven gods of luck and good fortune. There are also a few phallic deities and symbols.

The devotion accorded these deities is simply expressed. The devout passerby will pause before an image, clap his hands, bow in silence, and then resume his journey. He may toss a stone, hoping that, if it comes to rest on the image, it will bring him good luck. If some nearby shrine has placed an offering box by the image, he may contribute a coin. When a particular image becomes popular, and therefore a lucrative source of income, a shrine may move the image within its precincts or put up a small structure to protect it, thereby attracting more attention. In many cases a straw rope with paper cuttings attached marks it off as a sacred object. This is particularly likely to be the case if the object is a tree or stone. Such shrines are not included among the shrines of organized Shrine Shinto.

Spirit or demonic possession, necromancy, black magic, witchcraft, and purification rites are very popular among the common people. Attention must be called to the fact that these are all to be found in various forms within the practices of the established institutions and sects. But they also exist quite independently. There are, moreover, forms of the above which are distinctly Buddhistic, though generally these practices are identified with Shinto.

The persons who claim to possess occult powers—usually old women—are to be found in almost all small communities, especially in rural areas. They are consulted concerning queer feelings, odd sensations, and strange behavior. Many of these are regarded as witches by the superstitious. They call the spirits of dead or absent people into their presence and converse with them. People who are mentally unbalanced or actually insane are believed to be suffering some sort of spirit possession— the spirits usually being those of foxes, dogs or cats—and weird practices are resorted to by witches in attempts to cure them of their disabilities.

Of an entirely different nature are the rituals connected with the purification of plots of land to be used for construction. These are performed before the earth is broken in order to appease the spirit of the land, and such ceremonies are probably derived from worship of an earth deity.

It is not easy to draw the line between pure Shinto beliefs and general superstitions which appear to be of foreign origin. The unlucky corner which has to be guarded, the curved roof and the broken bridge, unlucky days and years—all these belong to the general folklore imported from China early in Japan's history. Generally speaking, however, Shinto ideas seem to predominate in Japanese necromancy and witchcraft, and, when witches call upon the spirits of the dead and exercise their occult powers, they usually invoke the deities of Shinto mythology. It is naturally impossible to estimate the number of people engaged in black magic and occult practices, but it is safe to say that faith in magic and sorcery is traditionally strong throughout the nation, especially among the less-educated people.

7

SHINTO: SHRINE

Shrine Shinto, like all other Shinto, originated in nature and spirit worship. Shrines themselves were rare in ancient times since natural objects such as mountains, rivers, islands, or forests were worshipped directly. It was only natural, however, for worshippers to build shrines for their deities, and soon there were small shrines dotting the countryside. Some were merely shelters under which a worshipper might stand in inclement weather, while others were built to enshrine substitute spirits and objects of worship.

Many of the present-day shrines are survivals from the ancient forms of nature worship. At the Suwa Shrine in Nagano prefecture, for instance, a forest is enclosed by a sacred fence and worshipped. Many shrines at the foot of mountains were originally nothing more than worship halls in which the worshipper would stand while saying his prayers to the deities dwelling on the mountain tops. But, when clan and ancestral deities (including mythological ancestors) became central in communal life, differentiation appeared among the objects or deities worshipped in certain localities and special shrines were built for dedication to the deities of local cults. Influences of one sort or another, especially ancestor worship from China, entered into this worship and caused the distinctions to be accentuated. The dominance of the Yamato clan resulted in the ascendancy of the

Sun Goddess and the shrine dedicated to her at Ise over other clan deities and shrines.

Buddhism dominated the shrines for a thousand years through dual-aspect Shinto and none escaped without showing some effects of this amalgamation with the foreign religion. There were also certain types of shrines, especially those devoted to nature deities and certain primitive guardian deities, which were greatly affected not only by Buddhism but by additional foreign influences, particularly Taoism, Chinese dualism, and shamanism. It was among these that the greatest changes occurred as the seeds of renascent Shinto developed in the eighteenth and nineteenth centuries. Some shrines were affected less than others by the religious upheaval of the Meiji Restoration, depending upon the degree to which they had been subjected to foreign influences.

The primary aim of the government in sponsoring Shrine Shinto after the restoration of imperial rule was to make the cult of the Sun Goddess and emperor worship pre-eminent among Shinto rituals. Due to government influence, a nationalistic trend began to characterize certain shrines more than others, and the element of emperor worship was added to their functions. This was especially true of many ancient shrines such as Ise, and of newer shrines built after the Restoration such as Meiji and Yasukuni, but even these sanctuaries could trace their ideological roots to primitive nature and spirit worship. It was their connection with "pure" Shinto and the most ancient of traditions which made them the tools of militaristic aggrandizement and the symbols of ultranationalism.

Shrine Shinto as a religious organization was a product of the modern era and did not exist until after 1868. When the new government failed in its attempt to make Shinto the official state religion, it set about to regiment all other religions and selected certain shrines to be placed under its direct supervision. These were classified in accordance with newly established categories and were placed under the Home Ministry, which proceeded to manage them in order to further the objective of creating a national cult based on Shinto. These specially selected shrines constituted the shrine system which is usually referred to as Shrine Shinto.

Shrine Shinto was declared to be non-religious, but it was treated as supra-religious. That is, it transcended all religions. Undesired elements were eliminated. Shrines were taken away from the control of families which had served them for centuries, and government officials were placed in charge. The custom developed of making one priest responsible for several shrines even though the shrines themselves had very little in common. In suppressing the religious element in the shrines, the special characteristics of each shrine were minimized as much as possible. For example, the order of service for ceremonies and festivals and the ritual prayers were all prepared by the government. Political or military friends of officials were often made priests. Everything tended to become secondary to the worship of the Sun Goddess and loyalty to the emperor and the state. Interviews with Shinto priests indicate that those who had the interests of their shrines at heart were not satisfied with bureaucratic control and the complete subjection of shrines to political and military ends.

Shrine Shinto today consists of some 110,000 shrines which were formerly under the control of the Home Ministry. These were sponsored and partly supported financially by the government, although contributions from the people have always constituted the bulk of their income. At present, all relations with the government have been severed. No longer supported or sponsored by the state, the shrines which were formerly associated with Shrine Shinto are free to develop like all other religious bodies, entirely dependent for support on the people. Some 86,000 of these shrines are now affiliated with a postwar organization known as the Shrine Association, and the rest are either members of small, local associations of shrines, are independent, or have ceased to exist except perhaps as dilapidated structures nestling in groves along the highways or hidden in the wooded slopes of mountains.

The Priesthood

From 1868 to 1945, the priests of Shrine Shinto were government officials. Some were trained in their duties and were educated in regular classical schools. The majority of the 16,000 priests who were active before and during the war were not so trained. Only about 10 per cent were educated in special schools like the Kokugakuin in Tokyo or the Kogakkan at Ise. Middle school graduates were given a special two-year course in ritual and classical literature, but many priests were given positions when they were retired from the army, with no special training other than short courses of instruction.

Priests were graded and given court rank according to the shrine they served. They were classified as follows: chief priests (*guji*), assistant chief priests (*gon guji*), ritualists (*negi*), and conductors (*shuten*). There was also an organization of priests,. the *Jingi Kai* (literally, Divine Affairs Society), but it was a formal, officially-sponsored organization for the purpose of carrying out the wishes of the government and arranging minor matters, such as wedding fees, on a non-competitive basis. Government officials were always the presidents. The chief priest of the highest ranking shrine in any given area was always the head. It was in no sense an association of priests carried on by the priests for their mutual benefit. Priests were paid approximately as much as school teachers, and perquisites of office helped to supplement this amount. Since all rituals and prayers were composed by the Home Ministry for the shrines and all major policies were made by the local government officials, the Home Ministry, or the Shrine Board, little was left to the initiative of the individual priests. Today, of course, the priests are no longer government officials.

Shrine Buildings

A Shinto shrine almost invariably consists of at least two main units, a main sanctuary (*honden*) and an oratory (*haiden*), with perhaps one or more auxiliary buildings, depending on the size of the shrine. There is almost invariably a *torii* and an ablution basin near the shrine. But even these things are not essential. Sometimes, in small or unimportant shrines, there is no oratory. In certain cases, there is no main sanctuary, because the object of worship itself is visible from the worship pavilion. The main sanctuary houses the object of worship, but, when this object is a mountain, sea, or some smaller object such as a rock or tree, only an oratory is required. In primitive times, there were no buildings of any sort, and only a straw rope with small paper or cloth cuttings attached to it enclosed the sacred object to guard it from pollution.

To a surprising degree, the Shinto shrines of the present day adhere to the architectural designs of primitive shrines. They are very simple and dignified. Straight lines prevail, and the timbers are unpainted. When there is elaborate ornamentation or color, it is due entirely to foreign influence. The usual ornaments in a shrine are branches of the sacred *sakaki* tree with white paper cuttings or long strips of cloth in five colors hanging

119

from it, and a mirror, sword, or beads. Reed curtains and cloth hangings are sometimes seen at the entrances or before the inner sanctuary, which is never open to the public.

Worship

Shrine worship is a very simple procedure. The devout individual who plans to go to a shrine to pay homage or worship will take a morning bath, put on clean clothes, perform his morning devotions before the god-shelf, and report his plan to go to a shrine. Then he will start out to the shrine.

Long before he approaches the shrine itself, he will have passed under a *torii*. This is both a means of purification and a barrier to entrance if he has any cuts, ailments, or other defilements; the sacred precincts of the shrine must not be polluted by blood or disease. Feeling a touch of the divine, he plods along the rough stones, the crunching beneath his feet being a kind of austerity which prepares his mind and body for worship.

Passing through one or more *torii*, he will pause at the ablution basin to wash his hands and rinse his mouth. A coin of appreciation to the water god may be dropped in a contribution box or tossed into the basin. He then proceeds toward the oratory. As he enters the gate to the inner precincts, he removes his hat, coat, and scarf. These and any parcels will be left to one side on a stand or on the ground. Facing the main sanctuary from outside the oratory, he will bow, throw a coin in the offering box, clap his hands twice, and pause with bowed head in an attitude of prayer. He then moves quietly away.

If he wishes to give more time to his devotions, he will go to the shrine office at one side, sign a registry book, and express a desire to enter the oratory to pay homage. Money for this will be given to the priest. Proceeding to the shrine, he will stand in the oratory where a priest will wave a branch of the sacred *sakaki* tree (or a paper imitation) several times before him and at each side for purification. Then, stepping forward, he will take a symbolic gift (*gohei*) and place it on the table facing the sanctuary. After clapping his hands twice and pausing a moment in silence, he will depart. He may return to the window outside the shrine office to buy a charm to ward off disease or bring good fortune, or he may draw lots from a box in order to determine what his future will be. As he passes out through the gate or *torii*, he will turn around and make a deep bow before returning to his home.

Types of Shrines

Shrines from time immemorial have been the affair of the common people. As a rule, they spring from the spontaneous movement of people who have become convinced that some person, object, natural phenomenon, or idea should be worshipped. The clan god was the result of venerating some illustrious leader or ancestor, historical or mythological, who was believed to possess divine power. The clan chiefs usually promoted such movements. The patron god, likewise, grew out of the people's interest in deities who were regarded as guardians or patrons of some skill or occupation or whose activities affected the daily life of the people. Thus, the farmer would become interested in one group of deities, the tradesman or craftsman in another, and travelers in still another group. There would naturally be some overlapping and duplication of functions.

But, while shrines have been primarily the expression of the common people, clan and government interest has resulted in the promotion of certain shrines for political motives. This was true in the early centuries and especially true in prewar years, when the government was using religion to control and indoctrinate the people.

There are several ways of classifying shrines, but none are very satisfactory. The Grand Shrine of Ise stood apart from all the rest in isolated splendor. Officially listed in addition to the Grand Shrine of Ise, there were 89 national, 27 special national, 87 state, 49,480 prefectural, district, or village shrines, and some 63,000 designated as shrines without rank. "Shrines without rank" was itself a classification. In addition to these there were thousands of small, uncounted, and officially unrecognized shrines.

National and special national shrines received gifts for presentation to the enshrined deities directly from the Imperial Household Department. State shrines received similar offerings from the national treasury. There was no distinction as to the deities, except that all the special national shrines were devoted without exception to the spirits of those who had rendered meritorious service to the emperor and the state. As the names indicate, the prefectural, district, and village shrines were supervised by local government officials and received token grants from local government treasuries. The shrines without rank received no regular financial support from any government office but were sponsored nevertheless by local government officials. These shrines were sacred to mythical gods, patriots, and heroes, phenomena and objects of nature, and various animals and objects, but it was seldom that any shrine was devoted exclusively to any of these.

In general, it can almost be said that shrines are all very much alike. While each shrine has its own name and a more or less clearly defined pantheon of its own, there is so much confusion regarding the enshrined deities that it apparently makes very little difference what the deities or objects enshrined really stand for. Shrines are essentially a medium whereby the wor-shipper, who in most cases is only vaguely aware, if at all, of the nature of the object enshrined or of the deities, gets in touch with the unseen. A priest feels free to invoke aid of any deity in the universe in order to meet the needs of a parishioner. More-over, priests—even professionally trained priests—are not ex-clusively devoted to the service of any one deity or group of deities or even a given type of shrine. Except in rare cases, they are quite willing to serve anywhere at any shrine. This is the result of the government policy and not necessarily a character-istic of the shrines themselves. In the following respects, then, shrines are alike. All shrines are symbols of man's relation to the unseen world of nature, ancestors, and the universe. Neither priests nor worshippers pay much attention to the specific nature of the shrines where worship is performed, although local shrines may retain reputations for efficacy in certain matters such as healing and divination. For general purposes, one shrine is as satisfactory as another. This was due to the special emphasis placed on the nationalistic nature of the shrines and the de-emphasizing of their religious significance.

There are, of course, certain shrines dedicated to historical individuals such as Emperor Meiji, General Nogi, Hideyoshi, Sugawara Michizane, or to groups of individuals such as the war dead enshrined at Yasukuni and the Gokoku shrines. There are also shrines which are dedicated only to mythological deities, an example being the Grand Shrine of Ise dedicated to the Sun Goddess. But these are very rare. Most shrines have pantheons all their own which often include deities with different or even contradictory characteristics.

Pantheism defies classification by its very nature. Every object is a deity or the expression of a deity, and, in the passage of years and in movement from place to place, those deities which survive acquire a peculiar eminence in the pantheon, take on new characteristics, and are identified with newly conceived or re-discovered deities often totally different in nature from the sup-posedly original deity. As time passes, a heretofore major deity sometimes becomes less significant or even disappears. The Hachiman and Inari shrines are good examples of the indefinite-ness of the deities to which shrines are dedicated.

Hachiman shrines are generally thought of as being dedi-cated to the god of war. But Hachiman has now become a fishing and agricultural deity. The basis for this shift is increased interest in a mythological imperial ancestor, Hikohoho-demi, an insignificant tutelary deity of fishermen who for centuries has been deified and identied with Hachiman. Hachiman has also been identied as the god of the forge or the patron of the primitive producers of spears and arrows and crude agricultural imple-ments. Hachiman (literally, eight-banners), while commonly thought of as originating in the custom of carrying banners into battle, is believed by some to indicate shamanistic origin, the banners being those set up when deities were invoked. The banner-poles acted as "conductors" whereby the invoked deities found their way into the presence of the worshippers. In the Nara period, Hachiman was made the guardian god of Buddhism. Later he was identified with the Buddha Amida, and his name was said to symbolize the eight-fold path of Buddhist morality. His connection with Buddhism proved very advantageous. When the capital was moved to Kyoto, the devotees of Hachiman estab-lished a shrine there. Then, because Hachiman was the tutelary deity of the Minamoto clan, another shrine was built when the military government was set up at Kamakura. From that time on, this deity has definitely been considered the chief patron of military men. Hence, Hachiman is sometimes inaccurately described as the god of war, but there is no denying that Hachiman shrines have been militaristic. Their popularity in wartime is sufficient evidence of this. But the present transformation of Hachiman into a peaceful god is entirely in accord with pantheistic practices.

Inari shrines are even more baffling. It is not sufficient to say that Inari shrines are dedicated to the goddess of food and fertility, or to designate them merely as "fox shrines." Inari shrines are dedicated to as many as nine main deities and ten subsidiary deities, not to mention additional names and variants. Each deity has diverse functions, and it is this diversity of functions among the deities which makes Inari shrines popular with different groups such as shopkeepers, manufacturers, farmers, and barren women. For the same reason, a small Inari shrine can be used to enhance the waning prestige of a larger shrine dedicated to a different deity. In the precincts of the Tsurugaoka-Hachiman Shrine in Kamakura, there is an Inari shrine which until now has been subordinated to the main shrine. With Hachiman's influence in question, the shrine now finds that it is Inari which is attracting an increasing number of visitors. Perhaps in the future the Inari shrine will take precedence over the Hachiman. This being the case, classification on the basis of the pantheon can be of little value.

One method of approaching the study of Shrine Shinto would be to examine enshrined objects, but it should be emphasized that while it is possible to study shrines on the basis of the objects worshipped, the enshrined objects are not necessarily a clear indication of the nature of the shrines. Mirrors, swords, stones, tablets, images, trees, mountains, caves, waterfalls, pigeons, and animals such as the snake and fox are among the most common objects of worship. Although each one originally may have had a special characteristic, in many cases this has been lost. Furthermore, the objects of worship have very little to do with the character of the deities of the shrines.

Objects of worship are divided into two categories and are called either god-bodies (*shintai*) or substitute spirits (*mitama-shiro*). These terms are generally used interchangeably even though technically there is a difference. A god-body is itself an object of worship while a substitute spirit is the object in which the deity dwells when it is invoked. The use of these terms is very confusing. The mirror at the Grand Shrine of Ise is the god-body, yet the Sun Goddess is also the god-body and is said to dwell in the mirror. At the Yasukuni Shrine, where a sword is the object of worship, the sword is a substitute spirit. The spirits of the enshrined deities dwell above in a heavenly city and only come down to the inner sanctuary where the sword is enshrined when spirit-invoking services are held. Ordinarily, the spirits are not there, so the sword, as a substitute spirit, receives the worship of the devout.

Where stones, tablets, weapons, clothing, and so forth are enshrined, these are regarded as god-bodies or as divine symbols of the enshrined deity. Articles closely connected with enshrined deities may become god-bodies even if there is only a mythological connection. The god-body of the Kamakura-gu, for instance, is a piece of armor which the enshrined deity, the imperial prince Morinaga, is said to have worn in battle. With the introduction of Buddhism, image worship became popular, and wooden statues or pictures were introduced. It should be noted in passing, however, that the god-body, or substitute spirit, is never exposed to view. It is always kept in a tightly closed compartment. Hence, most worshippers and, in some cases, even priests do not know the nature of the enshrined object.

The Grand Shrine of Ise, with its 14 subsidiary shrines, stood in a class by itself at the apex of the shrine system. As the shrine of the imperial ancestress, it was the family shrine of the emperor, and, on certain occasions, he functioned as priest. Virgin princesses of the imperial family acted as chief priestesses of this shrine for centuries. With the family-state concept at the center of Japan's political philosophy, emperor worship and ancestor worship were combined at Ise. The government propagandized the Sun Goddess as not only the progenitrix of the Japanese race but of all races, and she was slowly being identified as creator and ruler of the universe. The cult of Amaterasu was being made the unifying principle of the shrine system. Throughout the country there are Shimmei (Divine Radiance) and Tenso (Heavenly Ancestor) shrines dedicated to the Sun Goddess, although these have no relation to Ise. The subsidiary shrines at Ise are dedicated to mythological ancestors, among whom are the three creator deities introduced from China by the compilers of the *Kojiki*.

There are a few shrines such as the Meiji, Omi, and Kashiwara Shrines devoted exclusively to emperors. There are even shrines dedicated to emperors who were so mistreated in their lifetimes that their vengeful spirits were believed to require appeasement. Some of these are very old, but, until recent decades, they were of no special importance. The aggrandizement of emperor worship is a modern phenomenon. Because of it, the Meiji Shrine was becoming the center of a special Meiji cult.

Of equal importance with Meiji Shrine in the eyes of the military leaders, and hence increasingly important in the minds of the people, was the Yasukuni Shrine on Kudan Hill in Tokyo and the Gokoku shrines throughout the land, which were dedicated to war dead. Yasukuni Shrine was under the direct supervision of the military, and more particularly the army, which guarded jealously its prerogatives and let no opportunity pass to enhance its prestige. Yasukuni and the Gokoku shrines were at first spirit-invoking shrines (*shokon sha*) established to console the spirits of the loyalists who died in bringing about the Restoration. Under nationalistic stimulus, however, they were predominantly used by the military to stir up the war spirit. From 1937, a major general was chief priest of Yasukuni, and military personnel were often found on the staffs of Gokoku shrines.

Shrine Shinto is thus an assortment of shrines which were specially chosen as centers for the development of the national cult. Under official tutelage, they were slowly being unified into a system which would eliminate the religious elements and make state ceremonies and festivals paramount. Special characteristics tended to disappear. There was no relationship between them so that, except for government officials, no leadership existed. When sponsorship by the government was stopped, the backbone of the old shrine system was broken.

8

SHINTO : SECTARIAN

Sectarian Shinto comprises a number of heterogeneous sects which the government by ordinance brought together into one classification. In 1882, the Meiji government divided religious organizations into three categories: Buddhist, Christian, and Shinto. For lack of a better classification, all institutions and organizations which were not associated with Buddhism or Christianity were classified as Shinto sects, and Shinto was divided into Shrine (*Jinja*) Shinto and Sectarian (*Kyoha*) Shinto.

The religious groups which became known as Sectarian Shinto organizations in 1882 were not necessarily connected with each other doctrinally. They were for the most part small groups centered about the faith and activities of living evangelists. To call them collectively Shinto was something of a misnomer, since, in some there were strong elements of esoteric Buddhism, Taoism, and primitive nature worship. In one, there was no Shinto at all. But the government, reluctant to let these sects get out of its control, regulated their activities and required them to meet certain conditions in order to receive approval and function as religions.

The roots of some of these Shinto sects are to be found in the ancient folkways of the Japanese race. The doctrines of others were purely original with the late Tokugawa period. Some are outgrowths of renascent Shinto, and still others owe their origin to the religious experiences and opinions of their founders. Most of them derived their inspiration from occult practices prevalent among priests of either Shinto or Buddhism.

In the first half of the nineteenth century, as the feudal government was beginning to crumble, many old religious practices and beliefs which had been neglected for centuries were revived. The interest in Confucian doctrines also gave rise to entirely original religious movements, and, by the time of the Meiji Restoration, there were many small groups which independently practiced faith healing, mountain worship, ancient purification rites, and pure nature worship. In spite of opposition from the established religions and even persecution, they thrived. When the new Meiji regime attempted to establish a theocratic Shinto state, these groups were persecuted and suppressed much in the same manner as was Buddhism. But the government failed at first to attain its objective of a national cult, and, after various attempts to keep these new religious groups under government control had failed, some were permitted to become independent sects.

The government managed to maintain a measure of administrative control, however, and looked with disfavor upon a multiplicity of sects. Accordingly, only 13 of these groups were granted recognition by the government as independent sects, although many others existed. The latter were left no choice but to join the recognized sects as orders. Since the end of the war and the establishment of religious freedom, all such restrictions have been removed, and a number of the groups which had been associated with established Shinto sects have become independent organizations. These cannot be dealt with here since they are too nebulous for accurate description. Their characteristics will be taken up in the following chapter. The present discussion will be limited to those organizations which, since the Meiji era, have been traditionally classified as sects of Shinto. But it should be remembered that their association with Shinto was in some cases due purely to arbitrary government classification.

The organizations associated with Sectarian Shinto can be divided into five groups. Some are pure Shinto sects, some are permeated with Confucian doctrines, some have their origin in mountain worship, some are based on ancient ceremones of purification, and some (of peasant origin) are interested principally in faith healing. Each sect has an independent ecclesiastical organization and holds its own legal properties. They are all more or less actively engaged in propagandizing their doctrines, publishing many books and periodicals which are mainly concerned with ethics and religion. Some are active in programs for social welfare and maintain numerous schools and employ religious educators. And, unlike Shrine Shinto, the sects conduct regular religious services with sermons and elaborate rituals. These are attended by large congregations.

However, there are some points of identity between Sectarian Shinto and Shrine Shinto. The deities worshipped are usually the same, although this is not always the case. Most of the Shinto sects selected various prominent deities from the pantheon of ancient Shinto which happened also to be prominent in Shrine Shinto worship. But some, while including a few deities from the primitive religions, invented new ones of their own. The Great Parent God of Tenri-kyo, for instance, is not to be found in old Shinto, and Konko-kyo has no Shinto deities at all.

Statistics on the number of adherents in Sectarian Shinto are not reliable. Some years before the war, they claimed collectively 17,000,000 followers. But it is doubtful if they ever had such strong support, because, in 1943, the government placed this figure at only 10,000,000. More recent figures obtained from sect headquarters support this government estimate and indicate that at present the adherents of Sectarian Shinto number roughly 10,000,000.

Many of the sects contain in their doctrines various ancient traditions and a strong flavor of nationalism, and it was thought that, under the influence of the ultranationalism which swept Japan just before and during the war, they might achieve greater popular support and vitality, but this apparently did not take place. They did not gain in prestige during the war, and, since the termination of hostilities, many have been thrown into confusion. Except for the three sects of peasant origin, there is no evidence that they can even hold their own. Those which depend on the peasant folk for support, however, appear to be improving their position, and Tenri-kyo is at present one of the most active religious organizations in Japan. In spite of the nationalism inherent in certain of these sects, there is little reason for believing they will have a reactionary influence.

Pure Shinto Sects

There are three sects which fall into this category: Tai-kyo, Shinri-kyo, and Taisha-kyo. None of these have authentic historical founders, and they simply perpetuate ancient practices and beliefs revived in the latter part of the Tokugawa era by patriots and students of religion. They are conservative and imbued with imperialistic loyalism, but in their re-interpretation of the ancient native religion they have been progressive. They have been flexible enough to make certain adjustments to the postwar world, yet most of these adjustments have been of a negative nature, and the number of their adherents is shrinking.

Each of these sects maintains that it is the real repository of pure Shinto as practiced in ancient times, and they all draw upon the *Kojiki, Nihongi,* and other old texts for their scriptures. The number of deities worshipped varies with each, but common to all three sects is the predominance of the great central figures of Shinto mythology such as the three deities of creation, the two parent deities of the Japanese race, and the Sun Goddess. Their doctrines are chiefly concerned with the divine intention and virtues of these deities and the duty of sinful man to lead a righteous life untainted by selfish desires. They stress the need of spiritual purification for the restoration of man's divine nature, and worshippers are enjoined to follow moral precepts, usually in the form of prohibitions, and are taught to cultivate virtues such as fortitude, loyalty to the state, secret charity, and compassion for the less fortunate. Especially prominent in their articles of faith are exhortations of loyalty to the emperor and gratitude to ancestors. Their basic aims are to make plain the "way of the gods" and to bring to full expression the inherently divine nature of the Japanese people.

Tai-kyo. From the very beginning Tai-kyo was nothing more than a great number of small religious groups of varying persuasions which by government regulation became loosely associated through a headquarters organization. There are said to be as many as 300 sub-sects, but the actual number is not known. The sect headquarters is in Tokyo, and Tai-kyo adherents are to be found throughout Japan. The 997 churches of the sect are organized administratively into two groups: those organized by prefectures under the headquarters, and those under the direct control of larger churches in the field. There are 5,289 priests and 1,091,078 adherents in Japan. Before the war Tai-kyo was very active in spreading its doctrines abroad through missionary efforts. In Hawaii, it had five missionaries and seven churches with congregations totaling 18,989 worshippers. In North America and Manchuria, it had five missionaries and four churches with congregations totaling 4,277 worshippers.

Shinri-kyo. In addition to the practices and beliefs common to the pure Shinto sects, Shinri-kyo encourages sacred writing and drawing, sacred music, dancing, flower arrangement, and the tea ceremony in order to stimulate national customs and preserve the ancient etiquette. Another point of departure is the inclusion in its pantheon of the modern founder of the sect. The headquarters of Shinri-kyo is in Fukuoka prefecture and almost all of its adherents are to be found in southwestern Japan, particularly in Kyushu. It is not very strong numerically and is the smallest of the three sects in this group. It has 297 churches, 4,187 priests, and 346,143 adherents.

Taisha-kyo. Taisha-kyo has the largest following of all the Shinto sects. Its head shrine in the Izumo area along the north shore of western Japan was built many centuries ago and the Senge family has held the hereditary office of high priest from earliest times. After the Meiji Restoration, the Shrine Bureau of the Home Ministry classed this head shrine as a national shrine, but the Senge family staunchly contended that its functions were essentially of a religious nature. Accordingly, the parishioners were listed as a religious body by the Bureau of Religious Affairs, and it is from this group that the present Taisha-kyo has developed. Since that time, the head of the Senge family has held both the sect leadership and the secular office of high priest in the national shrine, which is still regarded by Taisha-kyo adherents as its headquarters.

Although this sect worships the usual Shinto deities, its central deity is Okuni-nushi-no-mikoto, the ruler of paradise and the tutelary deity of agriculture, medicine, and marriage, to whom the great head shrine is dedicated. The sect lays special emphasis on the performance of rituals for the purpose of securing divine favor on special occasions such as births, marriages, and deaths. Its religious services consist of purification rites, preaching, and moral exhortation, and these are frequently conducted in hospitals and factories as well as in churches designed for the purpose. It is active in education and social welfare work. It maintains a high school, kindergartens, and a training school for teachers, and conducts festivals and exhibitions for the encouragement of agriculture, a consumers union, and bartering exchanges. The sect has altogether 367 churches served by 20,146 priests, and virtually all of its 3,404,983 adherents are to be found near Izumo in the southwestern part of Japan.

Confucian Sects

There are two Confucian sects: Shusei-ha and Taisei-kyo. They are not officially called Confucian sects but are classified as such for convenience here, because they openly encourage and preach Confucian doctrines in addition to their Shinto doctrines. Confucian ideas permeate the entire nation, of course, but they are not usually as clearly recognizable as they are in the teachings of these two schools. And as might be expected, being infused with the Japanese variety of Confucianism which exalts patriotism and practical nationalism, they are the most nationalistic of the Shinto sects.

Both Shusei-ha and Taisei-kyo worship the central deities of the Shinto pantheon and also the spirits of various priests and sainted believers, but it should be noted that the three deities of creation taken from the Shinto pantheon are identified with Jotei, the Confucian god. There is naturally much emphasis on the ethical doctrines of Confucius. The main purpose of those sects, however, is to give believers a clear understanding of the fundamental principles of Shinto so that it may flower in the thoughts and practice of the people.

Shusei-ha. This sect was recognized as the most patriotic of the Shinto sects before and during the war, but most of its ultra-nationalistic elements have been eliminated in postwar adjustments. Its churches have the appearance of being shrines, because they have the architectural features most characteristic of pure Shinto shrines, including the *torii* at the entrance to the compound. Believers rely on sincere prayer and the repetition of religious phrases in order to gain inner tranquility, achieve spiritual union with the deities, and fulfill their duties as imperial subjects. Particular stress is laid on the five cardinal relationships of society taught by Confucius. The sect has 385 churches, 1,676 priests, and 43,584 adherents, most of whom are in western Japan, although the sect headquarters is in Tokyo.

Taisei-kyo. Taisei-kyo almost makes a religion of practical nationalism. In addition to the Confucian ethics and ancient Shinto beliefs included in its doctrines, however, it encourages business enterprises, the study of sciences, and the arts. Its followers are enjoined to be loyal citizens, to promote national institutions, and to worship the spirits of successive generations of emperors. Taisei-kyo adherents engage in purification ceremonies, horoscopy, divination, fortunetelling, and rites of meditation, and practice control of breathing. Its scriptures are based on the *Kojiki* and *Nihongi* and the writings of its founder. All the buildings in its headquarters compound in Tokyo were destroyed by air raids, and the training school for teachers maintained there before the war is now inactive due to lack of facilities. Altogether there are 199 Taisei-kyo churches, 1,404 priests, and 135,000 adherents.

Mountain Sects

While the origin of Japanese mountain worship is undoubtedly hidden in the mysteries of antiquity, the earliest organized cult known in Japan came into being in the latter half of the sixteenth century when bands of pilgrims were organized on the basis of the teachings of a devout Fuji worshipper named Hasegawa. The three modern mountain sects represent continuations of the movement he started.

Jikko-kyo, Fuso-kyo, and Mitake-kyo are called mountain sects because their adherents believe the deities dwell in the mountains. Pious worshippers living in the valleys erect small shrines on every mountain peak to honor them and invoke their aid. Since the deities thus honored are essentially those of ancient Shinto, these sects and their minor branches are regarded as expressions of Shinto, but there is a strong admixture of Buddhist and Taoist influence in their practices, so that it is difficult to determine whether Shinto is really a proper designation for them. Most of their doctrines, however, are unmistakably based on those of Shinto, and their followers aim at attaining spiritual harmony with the deities through purification, religious austerities, and practice of the truth of Shinto in everyday life. They exalt the divine virtues of the deities and the benevolence of the imperial family. The eternal prosperity of the state, the welfare of mankind, and permanent peace are favorite themes in their teachings. Before the war, their doctrines included much that could be considered ultranationalistic, but most of these elements have been eliminated.

All mountains are believed to harbor spirits, but, for the nation as a whole, Mount Fuji is the most sacred. Some Japanese even consider it the creator-spirit of the whole world. A second popular favorite is Mount Ontake, the highest peak in the Japanese Alps. Originally, the adherents of the mountain sects were required to make pilgrimages to the tops of especially sacred mountains in order to purify themselves, but, for practical reasons, this is no longer required. However, devout believers who are able to do so still climb Mount Fuji and Mount Ontake to perform purification rites and other religious ceremonies.

Jikko-kyo. Jikko-kyo emphasizes practical activities rather than ritual and dogma. Believers are urged to demonstrate the inner spirit of the "way of the gods" in their daily conduct. They shun senseless argument and strive for simplicity and purity of all things. Universal brotherhood is one of their chief aims. Rites of divination and exorcism are sometimes performed by request, but certain groups within the sect frown on such practices. Mount Fuji is believed to be the holy dwelling place of the three Shinto deities of creation and is therefore the principal sacred mountain worshipped by Jikko-kyo adherents. The sect formerly maintained a training school for priests and a school for ascetic practices, but these were destroyed in air raids. The headquarters is in Tokyo, and there are 612 churches, 2,643 priests, and 221,038 adherents, many of whom live near the foot of Mount Fuji.

Fuso-kyo. Fuso-kyo is in many ways similar to Jikko-kyo, but it lays more emphasis on rituals and meditation. Its priests also practice divination, exorcism, and faith healing. Revelations from the three deities of creation residing in Mount Fuji are handed down to believers, and elaborate ceremonies are held for the reception of such revelations and for the annual opening of the path leading to the top of this sacred mountain. Worshippers are urged to pray for the prosperity and happiness of the nation rather than for their individual benefit, and they strive to attain inner tranquility and peace of mind through meditation on the virtues of the deities and their benevolence. The headquarters of Fuso-kyo is in Shizuoka prefecture and most of the sect's 463 churches, 3,049 priests, and 384,753 adherents are to be found in the Kanto region of Japan.

Mitake-kyo. Mitake-kyo is the largest of the mountain sects, and its adherents accord to Mount Ontake the same central position occupied by Mount Fuji in the worship of Fuso-kyo and Kikko-kyo. Devotees climb and worship the mountain all year round. Like those of the other mountain sects, Mitake-kyo practices include exorcism, divination, purification rites, and complicated ceremonies. Its believers and priests participate in elaborate ritual to celebrate the breaking of ground for buildings, the placing of ridgepoles in buildings, puberty, weddings, and funerals. Fire burning is the chief characteristic of Mitake-kyo purification rites. Believers are exhorted to manifest divine benevolence through love of fellowmen, to exalt the sacred virtues of the Shinto deities, and to be loyal citizens. They are also taught that the human soul returns after death to Mount Ontake, whence it came. The headquarters is in Nagano prefecture. Although all buildings in the headquarters compound were destroyed in air raids, new ones have been constructed. There are 861 Mitake-kyo churches, 9,533 priests, and 1,647,573 adherents. Most of these are in the Kanto, Chubu, and Kansai districts.

Purification Sects

There are two sects which may be classed as purification sects: Shinshu-kyo and Misogi-kyo. Ceremonial purity plays an important part in the lives of all Japanese. It is marked characteristic of old Shinto, and all sects have some form of purification, but, in Shinshu-kyo and Misogi-kyo, purification rites take precedence over all others. The deities worshipped by followers of these sects are those of ancient Shinto, their scriptures are based on the *Kojiki* and *Nihongi,* and the precepts for believers are similar to those of other Shinto sects aside from the special emphasis on ritualistic purification. Loyalty to the emperor, filial piety, diligence in the performance of duties, and practice of the "way of the gods" are the main themes of these precepts. The purification rites performed by these two sects are perpetuations of ceremonies instituted in the mythological age for the purification of the mind and body from evil.

Shinshu-kyo. Shinshu-kyo holds an extraordinary regard for ceremonial practices as a means of washing away evil and pollutions. Its other religious ideas are almost negligible. The main purpose of the sect is the perpetuation of what it considers to be genuine Shinto orthodoxy, and it has made no attempt through postwar adjustments to alter or modify its basic doctrines. Its principal rituals include a fire-subduing ceremony, a hot water ritual, a ceremony of the twanging of bowstrings, and a rice-cooking ceremony. These four are performed together with the recitation of prayers for purification of mind and body. There is another ceremonial practice for producing an ecstatic state of mind in order to commune with the deities. Divination and exorcism are also practiced. In addition to the central figures of the Shinto pantheon, believers worship Ame-no-minaka-nushi-no-mikoto, one of the three deities of creation, as the absolute spiritual source of all things. The sect headquarters is in Tokyo. There are 233 churches, 2,923 priests, and 401,000 adherents.

Misogi-kyo. The ceremonies of Misogi-kyo are derived from very ancient Shinto rites for the purification of the soul. Deep breathing is considered to contribute to physical and mental well-being, since breathing is an elementary function of man and the source of life. It is believed that the myriad sicknesses of mind and body arise from improper breathing. Adherents of Misogi-kyo are taught that for purification nothing excels the act of proper breathing and that, by it, one can commit the direction of one's life to the divine will. The ceremonies of this sect consist of rituals, preaching, and exhortations to moral living and dutiful citizenship. Special services are held in all churches on the twelfth day of each month to celebrate Founder's Day. The headquarters of the sect is in Tokyo and most of its adherents are in the Tokyo area. The sect has 46 churches, 777 priests, and 83,401 adherents.

Sects of Peasant Origin

All the sects discussed thus far have been definitely Shinto in origin in spite of having many non-Shinto elements. The three sects of peasant origin, however, are of an entirely different nature. Their connection with Shinto is slight, and they are classed as Shinto sects only because they were required to register as such with the government in order to be recognized as independent religious bodies. Some Shinto deities are worshipped, but, since the end of hostilities and the establishment of religious freedom, there have been indications of a tendency to drop the elements which bind them to Shinto.

Faith healing is one outstanding characteristic of these sects. They are, therefore, sometimes referred to popularly as faith healing sects, but this is not an adequate description. Nor is it truly accurate to call them sects of peasant origin, since the founder of Kurozumi-kyo was a descendant of the famous Fujiwara family. All three of these sects received their strongest support from peasant folk, however, and for this reason are classified here as sects of peasant origin.

The founders of these sects were inspired by original religious beliefs, and the rapid spread of their teaching can be attributed to their personal magnetism. They preached popular theism and taught that there is a divine power which is the source of all life. This all-pervading power could be realized in human life, according to their doctrines, if all selfish motives and passions were conquered. They believed that inspiration could be received from the divine source through pure religious faith on the part of believers, and the question of who and what is divine was not considered so important, provided the individual recognized the divine qualities in himself and strove to realize this divine power in his everyday life.

The vital religious spirit which pervades these groups has made them the most active and influential of the Shinto sects. Their missionary activities are extensive, and considerable success was achieved before and during the war in their efforts to convert people in foreign countries. The ability they showed in adjusting themselves to the requirements of the postwar world is evidence that they will not die out in the foreseeable future.

Kurozumi-kyo. Kurozumi-kyo was founded by Kurozumi Munetada (1780–1850), whose family had furnished priests to Okayama prefecture for generations and had won the respect of the countryside. His father was the chief priest of a Sun Goddess shrine. Munetada was a deeply religious person who experienced three stages of spiritual development, each connected with a religious crisis in his life. The third occurred in 1814 and marked the beginning of his missionary work which resulted in the present sect named after him.

No systematic exposition of his thoughts was left by Munetada, but his letters, poems, and written observations are employed by the sect as sacred scriptures. Apparently, he was praying to the rising sun in 1814 when he received a sacred commission from the Sun Goddess herself to spread his faith to all people. He, therefore, began to preach obedience to the way of the Sun Goddess as the source of all joy and health. Other deities of the Shinto pantheon were included, but the Sun Goddess became the central deity of his faith. She was believed to be the universal, all-inclusive parent spirit of the universe, the source and sustaining guide of all things, the impartial benefactress of heaven and earth. It should be noted that Munetada's conception of the Sun Goddess differed somewhat from that of traditional Shinto. He also taught that his followers should live by the "Seven Rules of the Divine Law," a series of admonitions of faith, humility, self-possession, compassion, industry, gratitude, sincerity, and other virtues.

The doctrines of Kurozumi-kyo are based on the teachings of Munetada, who has himself been deified. He is now worshipped along with the Sun Goddess and other Shinto deities. The sect teaches the identity of man and god through the Sun Goddess and preaches universal brotherhood. Genuine faith healing is practiced and is supplemented by hypnotism. Therapeutic energy is magically transferred to ailing parts of the body by rubbing. Healing sometimes is accomplished by the recitation of purification rituals, and sometimes consecrated water is offered to the patient, or ejected upon the patient from the mouth of a priest, or ejected upon paper bearing the name of the patient.

Kurozumi-kyo is very active in spreading its gospel through propaganda. Faith healing is, of course, the chief attraction, but lectures and publications are employed, and, before the war, motion pictures were used for propaganda purposes. The sect has training schools for priests, is affiliated with a middle school, and manages 5 day nurseries, 50 children's clubs, 10 Sunday schools, and a young men's association with 90 branches. The headquarters is in Okayama prefecture, and most of the Kurozumi-kyo adherents are located in the territory west of Nagoya. In Japan, there are 433 churches, 3,409 priests, and 574,032 adherents. Before the war's end, there were 6 churches, 28 priests, and 2,712 adherents in Korea and Manchuria and one small branch in Sakhalin.

Konko-kyo. Konko-kyo was founded in 1859 by Kawade (1814–1883), an uneducated farmer who had a vision in which he was called to the sacred mission of being the medium of communication between mankind and the "great father of the universe." This deity, Tenchi-kane-no-kami, was invented by the founder and is not to be found in ancient Shinto. He is described as being the eternal sprit, the source of all beings and all things, the god of infinite mercy and love. The founder did not leave any of his teachings in writing, but his thoughts and sermons were compiled by disciples into sets of commandments and instructions, which are employed by the Konko-kyo as scriptures. Apparently, he taught that all men should believe in Tenchi-kane-no-kami and, through faith in him, love each other, pray for peace in the world, and fulfill their duties to self, family, and society in happiness and prosperity. Human suffering and calamities were attributed to ignorance of his love and violation of his laws. These became the basic doctrines of Konko-kyo.

In the early part of the Meiji period, three Shinto deities were adopted as manifestations of Tenchi-kane-no-kami in order to accommodate the government, which would not recognize the sect unless it had Shinto deities. When the sect registered in 1946 in accordance with the Religious Corporations Ordinance, however, these were dropped, and Tenchi-kane-no-kami was listed as the only deity worshipped. Followers of Konko-kyo pay special reverence to the founder, also, but he is not deified.

Konko-kyo has advanced farther than any of the Shinto sects in freeing itself of the restrictions of traditional ceremonies and superstitions. It repudiates popular magic, divination, exorcism, ascetic practices, and ostentatious rituals. It relies for strength on the creative spiritual power of its believers. The function of the church is to supply an intermediary service through which man and god become indivisibly united and the salvation of man is realized.

Konko-kyo, like the other sects in this category, is active in missionary and social welfare work. It maintains a training school for priests and teachers, a boy's high school, a library, a girl's high school, and a scholarship aid association. The headquarters of the sect is in Okayama prefecture and most of its 683,036 adherents are in southeastern Japan. It has 1,540 churches served by 2,637 priests. Konko-kyo also maintained missions overseas, and though the confusion following the war made contact with these missions difficult, there were at one time as many as 65 churches with 46,063 adherents in Korea and Manchuria, and 32 churches with 10,095 adherents scattered through the Orient in Sakhalin, Formosa, Central and North China, Hawaii, Singapore, and Hong Kong.

Tenri-kyo. Tenri-kyo is without doubt the most active and influential of all the Shinto sects. It was founded in 1838 by a woman, Nakayama Miki (1798–1887), and the office of chief priest has been held by her direct descendants to the present day. The emphasis laid on faith healing by Tenri-kyo and the fact that it was founded by a woman has given it some resemblance to Christian Science, but there are no other points of similarity.

Tenri-kyo doctrines are based on the assumption that this is a reasonable universe and that the ultimate reality is divine reason. He who lives according to reason shall prosper, and he who violates reason shall perish. God wills that all men shall enjoy happiness and prosperity in this life, but man, moved by selfish desires and wicked thoughts, suffers misfortune and disease. Man can only progress spiritually by casting out evil. All evils, referred to as "dust," are related to greediness, stinginess, misguided love, hatred, selfishness, spite, and anger. By gaining mastery over these "dusts" within him through faith in God and trust in his benevolence, man can at last reach contentment. When the union between man and God is perfect, divine favor will cure illnesses, turn unhappiness into joy, and save the soul.

Another noteworthy Tenri-kyo teaching is the doctrine of causality. Unfortunately for man, virtues and "dusts" may have been accumulated in a previous existence so that the circumstances of this life are completely beyond prediction. The sect believes in reincarnation, and its fundamental purpose is to change all men into virtuous agents. In this connection, the negation of "dusts" does not suffice, and man must strive earnestly to remove all wicked elements in society and serve his fellowmen while serving God faithfully. In this way, the ideal "kingdom of peace" will be achieved.

The activities and institutions of Tenri-kyo are the most numerous and significant in Sectarian Shinto. In the field of education, the sect has two advanced language schools, two middle schools for boys and one for girls, training schools for priests, elementary schools, several kindergartens, libraries, many dormitories for students and pilgrims, and numerous lecture halls both at headquarters and in the local churches. The headquarters in Nara maintains a school for missionaries where many foreign languages, including English, French, German, Spanish, Malayan, and Chinese, are taught to prepare for the conversion of the entire world. In the headquarters compound, there is a spot selected as the location for the "terrace of nectar" which is to be built when the whole world is converted. This spot is believed to be the very place where man originated.

In the field of social service, Tenri-kyo gives practical support to its idealism through clinics, a tuberculosis sanitorium, the Tuberculosis Research Institute, orphan asylums, occupational training agencies, and day nurseries. Many of its churches support various types of social welfare organizations. Tenri-kyo adherents do voluntary labor as proof of their determination to carry into actual practice the ideals of their faith. Believers contribute labor to public services, working in groups to clean city streets, erect shelters for the homeless, and render other useful services to their communities. This participation in public activities not necessarily related to their churches has been an important factor in obtaining popular support for their religion.

The deity worshipped by Tenri-kyo followers is Tenri-o-no-mikoto, the god of divine reason, a composite deity made up of ten Shinto deities. The religion of these people appears to be a living force. Faith healing, public services, and the strong central organizations of the church have accounted for the rapid growth of Tenri-kyo, especially in the last 30 years. A well-organized administrative system keeps all churches in close contact with the mother church in Nara, and all branches of Tenri-kyo act in harmony on matters of policy, thereby presenting a united front in a common cause. This directness of purpose has made Tenri-kyo one of the most vital religious forces in Japan. In addition to its 11,978 churches, 76,315 priests, and 1,158,414 adherents, it has a strong following abroad, principally in south-eastern Asia. There are more than 530 overseas churches.

9

CHRISTIANITY

Early Christianity in Japan

Japan's first direct contact with Christianity was in 1549 when Francis Xavier, accompanied by two other Spanish Jesuits, arrived in Kagoshima, the southernmost prefecture on the island of Kyushu. They and subsequent missionary groups were allowed to preach freely and soon made some converts; but this tolerance of the new religion seems to have stemmed not so much from an eager embracing of Christian tenets as from a mistaken belief on the part of the Japanese that, because of certain similarities in ritual, it was another of the many heretical sects in Buddhism, and also from the fact that the missionaries were invariably accompanied by traders with exotic commodities. Numerous local lords encouraged the propagation of Christianity in their fiefs and ordered their people to treat the missionaries with respect and, in some extreme cases, to embrace Christianity en masse. Sometimes, when no ships or traders came, these lords ordered their fiefs to revert to their former faith. What few voluntary converts the missionaries were able to make were people of the lower classes to whom charity and medical care had been extended.

Xavier had realized that the patronage of the imperial court would sway the people to this new religion and had proceeded to Kyoto, then in a chaotic state with various factions contending for power; but he was unable to see anyone of consequence. Xavier left Japan in 1552. His successors made slow headway among the upper classes, who were impressed by the learning and the striking appearance of the missionaries. Their influence was vigorously opposed by the Buddhist priests, who were then all-powerful and who meddled in secular affairs, until the missionaries were received by Oda Nobunaga, the first of three great leaders who succeeded in uniting Japan. Nobunaga, then in the midst of a campaign to break the power of the Buddhist monasteries in Kyōto, took kindly to this new doctrine. He was also desirous of securing avenues for foreign trade. Under his patronage, the Christian faith made fair progress, and, in a report sent to Rome by the Jesuits in 1582, there were said to be 80 missionaries and a total of 150,000 converts.

Nobunaga was succeeded by Toyotomi Hideyoshi, who came to power in 1582 and who continued to favor Christianity, but not for long. In 1587, he suddenly issued an edict banning the missionaries from Japan, but he did not enforce this edict with any severity until ten years later when, viewing the dissension between the Jesuits and the Franciscans and alarmed by the conviction that missionaries were the forerunners of political intrigue and aggression—a belief bolstered and strengthened by the Protestant traders from Holland and England who began to come to Japan to trade in increasing numbers from the beginning of the seventeenth century—he began a campaign to oust the missionaries and to suppress Christianity. This persecution culminated in the execution in Nagasaki of 6 Spanish Franciscans, 3 Jesuits, and 17 Japanese converts. Only the death of Hideyoshi and the subsequent struggle for power diverted attention away from the persecution of Christians and brought respite to the missionaries.

Hideyoshi's successor, Tokugawa Ieyasu, the founder of the

Tokugawa dynasty of hereditary military rulers, was as eager for foreign trade as had been his two predecessors, and he was inclined to be tolerant of the new religion at first; but the suspicions entertained by Hideyoshi toward the motives of the missionaries grew to such an extent in Ieyasu that, in 1614, after a series of mild warnings, he issued an edict which led to the imprisonment, torture, and death of missionaries and converts. Hundreds of converts were banished from their homes. There were numerous Christian martyrs among the Japanese converts who held to their faith with tenacity and died for it. Some of them smuggled missionaries into Japan at a time when discovery meant a cruel death. Just as no reliable figures are available as to the number of Christians in Japan during the first quarter of the seventeenth century (they vary from 300,000 to 750,000), so there are no accurate figures on the number of martyrs who went to their deaths. But thousands of converts, for the most part peasants, died for their belief. The most spectacular event at this time, one which was an immediate reason for closing of Japan to the world, was the uprising of October, 1637, when several thousand Christians on the island of Amakusa and on the Shimabara Peninsula, near Nagasaki, rose up in arms against persecution and held out for months in siege against the forces sent to subdue them, surrendering early in 1638. Over 30,000 converts, including women and children, were massacred. Those who clung to their faith were put to the sword; those who were lukewarm in their faith apostatized. With the Shimabara massacre, Christianity, though it did survive underground in certain communities in Kyushu, was virtually brought to an end in Japan. For the next 200 years, Japan remained isolated from the rest of the world.

Christianity in Modern Japan

The second period in the history of Christianity in Japan begins when Japan was forced to open her doors to the West. Protestant Christianity was introduced, and missionaries were permitted to reside in Japan and to build churches in settlements for the spiritual welfare of the foreign residents. Nevertheless, the government, which had not lifted its anti-Christian edict, remained hostile to Christianity.

The first Catholic church was built in Yokohama in 1862. In the following year another was built in Nagasaki. In 1865, a group of Japanese entered the church at Nagasaki, recognized the cross and the statue of the Blessed Virgin, and approached the missionary. After questioning him about the doctrine he preached, the Japanese revealed to him that, in and around Nagasaki, thousands of them had kept alive the faith that their ancestors, cut off from the rest of the world and driven underground, had handed down to them.

The government, on learning that the Catholic faith which had lain quiescent for 200 years had revived, promptly arrested nearly 4,000 Japanese believers, on the ground that it would be dangerous to allow them to congregate in one area, and banished them to other feudatories until they expressed a willingness to renounce Christianity. Shortly afterward, the Tokugawa government collapsed.

With the restoration of the emperor in 1868, there was introduced the idea of setting Shinto up as the state religion. The government's stand against Christianity was one of unmitigated opposition, and notices forbidding the propagation of Christianity among the Japanese were published in the first year of Meiji.

The first Protestant missionaries who entered Japan at Nagasaki in 1859 were under strict police surveillance, being forbidden to preach among the natives. But propaganda was carried on covertly, and the first native Protestant covert was baptized in 1864. The first Protestant church was established in Yokohama in 1872, and, in the following year, the government lifted its edict proscribing Christianity and permitted the missionaries to preach freely. The Catholic exiles were released in the same year. But the anti-Christian sentiment did not abate until the 1880's when Japan realized that she had lagged behind the West in her isolation and would have to import Western civilization wholesale if she were to catch up with the rest of the world. At a time when all things Western were eagerly welcomed by the Japanese, Christianity was naturally carried in on the tide of popularity, and missionaries were welcomed as representatives of the new civilization.

In the last decade of the nineteenth century, a reaction against Christianity set in. The conflict between religion and science, the rising tide of nationalism in Japan, and the belief by Japan that the Western nations, in refusing to agree to the revision of earlier treaties on terms of equality, were not entirely Christian in their international dealings, caused Christianity to suffer a setback. Enthusiasm for Christianity waned when an indiscriminate admiration for things Occidental gave way to a strong conservatism and a national consciousness. Many converts deserted the Christian cause; but others sought to re-examine the deeper meaning of Christianity, and the opening of the twentieth century saw the pendulum gradually swinging back.

The third phase of Christianity in Japan begins at about this point. The idea of freeing the Christian church in Japan from foreign support and naturalizing it on Japanese soil was not new, and it was strengthened with the formation of the Japanese Congregational, Presbyterian, and Methodist churches. The Russo-Japanese War of 1904–05 had given confidence to the

Japanese church as well as to the nation. The church felt it could carry on without outside support. This was premature. The rise of industrialism and its attendant emphasis on materialism caused alarm among religious bodies, and, in 1912, the Three Religions' Conference, comprising representatives of Shinto and Buddhist sects and Christian denominations, was called. At this meeting, recognition was given to the importance of religion in maintaining and improving the morals of the nation. Another aspect of this conference was the placing of the three religions on an equal footing, with virtual, though not as yet legal, recognition of Christianity as one of the religions of the land.

The first World War brought about a profound change in the life and thought of the Japanese. Great prosperity and the interpretation of the war as the breakdown of Christianity in the West caused a lull in Christian activities in Japan, but the humanitarian principles embodied in Wilson's Fourteen Points and the aid extended to Japan after the great earthquake of 1923 reawakened the people to Christianity. The passage by the United States Congress in 1924 of the Oriental Exclusion Act largely nullified this friendly atmosphere.

In the early 1930's, renewed attempts to unify the Japanese Protestant churches were made. Gradual reduction of subsidies and personnel from America and Europe threw the churches more and more on their own. A new emphasis was placed on evangelism for rural communities with the impetus provided by Toyohiko Kagawa, a well-known Japanese Christian leader. The Religious Bodies Law, an ordinance by which the Japanese government sought to bring all the religious organizations under closer supervision and which had been proposed in the Diet from time to time since 1934, was put into effect in April, 1940. In the implementation of this law, official recognition was given only to those religious bodies which had a membership of at least 5,000 and had 50 established meeting places. The smaller sects which were unable to meet these requirements joined other denominations. Although this law brought Christianity under greater surveillance than before, the government officially recognized the Christian church for the first time.

The movement toward union of the Japanese Protestant churches, which had not gone beyond the committee stage for 25 years, was now hastened under government pressure. By 1939, the "China Incident" was in its second year, and the government, particularly in the field of publications, was clamping down on the churches, which yielded to pressure and rallied behind the government. Separation from the Western churches was hastened, and, in this time of crisis, church activities were considerably diminished. In October, 1940, a mass meeting of Protestant denominations was held, and approval for the plan to form a united Protestant church was given. Shortly afterward, the various denominations were united in 11 blocs. In November, 1941, these blocs were federated, and the united organization known as the Church of Christ in Japan was made up of all the Protestant denominations. Part of the Episcopalian church and a few of the smaller churches, such as the Holiness church and the Seventh Day Adventist, which did not join, were not recognized as religious bodies but as religious associations; as such they were put under the supervision of the local police rather than under the Ministry of Education. Further pressure by the government erased all denominational lines and brought about a complete union, at least on the surface, in the Church of Christ in Japan in 1942.

This recognition by the government was of some value to the church during the war; but recognition did not minimize the suspicion and doubt thrown on Christians by the populace and the officials because of their previous close contact with the West.

Persecution of certain denominations occurred. The Holiness church, which finally joined the Church of Christ and the Seventh Day Adventist church, which did not, were ordered dissolved. The Salvation Army was ordered to revise its military terminology. The spy mania, abolishment of Sunday as a holiday, the evacuation of women and children from large cities, and the mobilization of pastors to munitions factories all caused a drop in church and Sunday School attendance. Services, however, were continued throughout the war, and the practices of bowing toward the imperial palace and praying for the soldiers who had died and for those at the front were generally added to the services. In 1944, the Church of Christ in Japan, along with the Roman Catholic Church, joined the Japan Wartime Patriotic Religions Association, in cooperation with the Shinto and Buddhist bodies.

With the end of the war the church was freed from government surveillance.

Christian Welfare Work

Social welfare work was not an entirely new thing in Japan when the Christian missionaries arrived. Mention of relief work for famine-stricken inhabitants is made as far back as the sixth century A.D. Buddhism, with its doctrine of compassion, gave early rise to relief work, and, down the centuries, temples and priests carried on welfare work.

The Jesuits who came to Japan in the sixteenth century had considerable success in their missions. They established hospitals, infirmaries, orphanages, and leper settlements in several localities. They established schools, brought in Western science, and taught astronomy, geology, meteorology, mathematics, and medicine. But this start was cut short when Catholicism was, for all practical purposes, exterminated in Japan after 1640, and Japan shut herself up in isolation for the next two hundred years. With the reopening of the country in 1859, the educational and social work pioneered by the Catholics was continued, joined by that of the Protestants. Modern scientific knowledge and methods strengthened and further stimulated interest in social work. Many of the early missionaries carried on relief work in connection with other activities, while some gave their entire time to it. Many of the early Protestant missionaries who entered Japan in the middle of the nineteenth century worked as medical doctors and propagators of the new sciences. They were influential in penal reform, temperance, nursing, and modern medicine. In later years the field was broadened to include the relief of extreme poverty, the provision of health services for the very needy, education for the underprivileged who could not attend ordinary schools, dormitories for young working women and for casual laborers, unemployment relief, establishment of kindergartens and day nurseries for children of working mothers, relief for families living in canal boats, and encouragement of education for organized laborers were among the most common forms of service. With the rise of industrialism at the start of the twentieth century, there was an increase in the attendant social evils. The missions, augmented by the coming of the Salvation Army to Japan in 1895, played an important part in combatting these evils. The Salvation Army was active in the prohibition campaign and in the movement to free inmates of brothels. As interest in social betterment was gradually aroused, the Japanese government and the community as a whole contributed materially to forwarding the projects, and, as highly trained personnel were necessary, many Japanese were sent abroad to study and observe and to return as trained workers.

The earlier stages in the propagation of Christianity and in social work naturally centered around the densely populated urban area; but, beginning in the 1920's, a movement for rural evangelism and rural social service came into effect, with Kagawa as the outstanding exponent with his Farmers' Gospel School. It was estimated in 1930 that about one-half or 35,000,000 of Japan's population lived in the 12,000 villages in the rural areas and along the seacoasts—villages which had hardly been touched by Christianity. The Farmers' Gospel School in Japan had as its aim the bringing of the spirit of Christianity to the rural areas. Despite all efforts, however, Christianity made little headway outside of urban areas.

No thorough study has been made of prewar social welfare institutions. Consequently, no satisfactory statistics are available regarding the work done. Before the war, the Catholic Church maintained 27 orphanages, 9 old people's homes, 16 hospitals and sanitariums, and 2 leprosariums. The Episcopal Church social welfare work was mainly in connection with two hospitals. The Protestant denominations maintained 18 social settlements, 11 medical clinics, 3 leprosariums, 3 old people's homes, 8 institutions for mothers and children, 12 orphanages, and 32 miscellaneous institutions, totaling 92 in all.

Christian Education

Christianity has throughout most of its history laid great emphasis on education. Japanese Christianity is no exception to this rule. Christian education may be considered in two major aspects: first, Christian schools; and second, the program of popular religious education carried on by the churches.

After Japan was opened to foreign intercourse, mission schools opened their doors. Two decades after the Meiji Restoration, when the importation of Western civilization was at its height, Christianity in Japan was having its heyday. The popularity of

157

mission schools was no doubt in part due to the fact that they offered an opportunity for acquaintance with Western culture, through their Western teachers, mostly American; but nevertheless, they had the opportunity to surround their students with Christian influence and to give a measure of Christian teaching.

The greatest contribution of the Christian school has been to the education of girls and women. From the time of the opening of the first school for girls in Japan in 1870 to the time when government schools for women were being promoted around 1900, the history of education for women in Japan is almost identical with the history of the Christian schools for girls. In 1905, Christian high schools for girls represented 70 per cent of the total number of girls' schools. However, by 1930, government education for women had advanced to the point where the Christian schools totaled less than 5 per cent. Just prior to the war, there were 59 Christian high schools for girls in Japan— 33 Protestant and 26 Catholic.

Since the Japanese government provided more generously for the education of boys than girls, the record of Christian boys' schools is not so favorable as that for girls. Yet just before the war there were 23 such schools—15 Protestant and 8 Catholic.

In the field of higher education there were 4 Christian universities and 23 colleges. Most of these were vocational in character, training students for commercial careers rather than for professions.

Christian churches have given considerable attention to the establishment of kindergartens, and this has been a fruitful field of service in view of the fact that the Japanese school system does not normally provide kindergarten education. It is in the field of the elementary school that Christian efforts have been least pronounced, there being not over 10 or 12 such schools under Christian auspices in Japan.

CHRISTIANITY

Christian education in Japan has been negatively influenced by two factors: first, the tendency of the Japanese government to favor the graduates of government schools over those of private schools, thus influencing those students who could pass the government examinations to seek admission to the government schools; second, the severe restriction on the teaching of religion in Japanese education, requiring schools to depend largely on extracurricular activities and general Christian influence for their Christian effectiveness. The proportionately large number of Christian men and women in the leadership of Japan today attests to the success of the Christian schools in their primary work of Christian education.

10

NEW SECTS

While it is true that new religious sects have mushroomed to a remarkable extent since the war, it is difficult to find any reliable evidence of their strength or influence, and the exact number of the new and strange sects which have sprung up since the end of hostilities is not known. Furthermore, many of these so-called new sects were actually in existence prior to the war but were part of one or another of the officially recognized organizations.

Due to the prewar policies of the Japanese government, new sects were not permitted to become independent religions. Consequently, any religious leader with a new idea or a revelation had to find support within an established sect. If he could not gain admission for his doctrines in any such organizations, he was forced to carry on a somewhat precarious campaign underground, subject at all times to close surveillance by the police. Police records are filled with investigations of various obscure groups nominally attached to some one of the Shinto sects. To illustrate the difficulties encountered by small religious organizations in their struggle for existence, the Hito-no-michi (Way of Man) group first appeared as part of Mitake-kyo, later transferred to Fuso-kyo, was suppressed altogether during the war, and in 1947 was revived as the PL Kyodan.

Disregarding the question of whether or not a sect is new,

an examination of the reports received from 24 unclassified sects reveals that they fall into five classifications: monotheistic, henotheistic, Shinto-polytheistic, messianic, and those of definite Chinese influence. Except for the monotheistic group, the deities of these sects are varied. The deity worshipped in a sect is sometimes a particularly selected one, but sometimes a limited number of important deities are selected from the Shinto pantheon, and, in a few cases, the entire Shinto pantheon is worshipped. As a whole, they have a very strong Shinto flavor, although Buddhist and Christian influences are not entirely lacking. A very few of them reveal the influence of Confucianism and Chinese dualism.

As most of the founders are still living, the sects do not use scriptures. Some, however, use the writings of their founders for ethical instruction. The messianic sects have no documents whatsoever since their founders claim their teachings are based on revelations and guide their followers by means of oracles. It is, therefore, very difficult to determine the exact nature of their doctrines, but apparently their chief concerns are the promotion of morality and the establishment of peace and prosperity in the world.

Each sect has an independent ecclesiastical organization and carries on religious propaganda. Most of them employ religious teachers and maintain meeting places. Some of the smaller sects conduct their meetings in the homes of their founders. Some are able to manage schools and carry on social welfare activities. Few of these sects have any permanent property. Their income is derived from assessments (annual and special) and offerings from teachers and believers. If the sect practices divination, sorcery, or incantation, the charges for these services is an important part of their income. Funds are also raised by certain sects through the sale of tablets and charms.

Most of the new religious groups conduct services at appointed times and perform prayer, exhortation, and ritualistic adoration. Faith healing is a dominant interest in several of the sects. Many of them also publish literature for the ethical and religious guidance of the people, but no sect is adequately revealed through its publications. It has to be studied in action in order to be understood. For the present purposes only a general characterization can be given of the types of new sects which fall under the five classifications listed above.

Monotheistic Group

General Monotheistic Type. In the general monotheistic type, one god is the source of all existence and the creator of all phenomena of the universe. All men are children of this god, who wills them to enjoy happiness and health. Misfortune and diseases result from violation of harmony with the real-self or the divine law of the universe. These sects teach believers (1) to believe in one god of the universe, (2) to cultivate morality in society, (3) to love their neighbors, and (4) to attain the welfare and peace of mankind. The teachings are very similar to those of Christianity, and special emphasis is placed on the brotherhood of man and ethical righteousness as the basis of everyday life. These sects do not perform any so-called Shinto magical practices, such as divination, sorcery, or incantation. Most of them have relatively large membership.

The sects which fall in this group are: Seicho-no-ie, Aizen-en, Daiso-kyo, Dokai-kyo, Seisei Kyodan, Renshindo, and Shidai Shindogyo-kai. PL Kyodan would also come under this group were it not for its artificial connection with Sectarian Shinto.

Composite Type of Christianity, Buddhism, and Shinto. Sects of the composite type claim that they have all the best elements of Shinto, Buddhism, and Christianity so as to make their teachings world religions. They wish to achieve harmonious life among the different races through belief in the one god who was revealed in all the religions of the world. Minsei-kyo is the most prominent of the sects which make up this group. The founder of Minsei-kyo makes it the purpose of his sect to do away with all the superstitious practices and formalism in religion.

Fusion of Shrine and Sect Shinto. The founders of Yuitsu Shinto and Tenso-kyo, the sects forming this group, have established a monotheistic Shinto by taking elements from Shrine and Sectarian Shinto. The sects place emphasis upon (1) harmony, (2) happiness, (3) love for neighbors, (4) courage, (5) sincerity, and (6) diligence. Divination, sorcery, and incantation are performed.

Henotheistic Group

With one exception, the henotheistic group of sects claims that the Sun Goddess is the source of all phenomena of the universe. Japan is blessed, because the Sun Goddess is the ancestress of the imperial family, and the way of the gods is one with the imperial way. They teach their followers to cultivate ethical righteousness in society and peace in the world through belief in the truth of the gods. They aim to unite the religions and cultures of the world through sun-worship. Various Shinto practices are performed.

The sects making up this group are: Yamato, Nichiren Kyosha, Tensho-kyo Hombu, Sugawara Kyodan, and Nikko Honkyo.

Shinto Polytheistic Group

The teachings of the Shinto polytheistic groups are typically those of Shinto. A limited number of the important gods, and in some cases the entire Shinto pantheon, are worshipped. Their teachings are centered on: (1) the principles of creation, and the development of the universe on the basis of the virtues of gods, (2) understanding of the significance of life and death through the truth existing indivisible both in the revealed and unrevealed worlds, and (3) purification from pollution of sickness, misfortune, and evil through the grace of the gods and repentance before the gods. In common with other sects, the founders exhort believers to live in accordance with the will of the gods and to contribute to the prosperity of mankind. The sects employ Shinto practices, (both ritual and magical.) Finger massage treatment is practiced in the Shimboku-kyo.

The sects which make up this group are: Shimboku-kyo, Shinri-kyo, Hinomoto Kyodan, Sumera-kyo, and Sumera-kyo Honin.

Messianic Group

According to Jiu-kyo and Kotai Jingu-kyo, the two sects in the Messianic group, the gods guide and direct human society through the revelation of a founder. The founder is the mediator between man and the Sun Goddess and is here on earth to give the grace of the Sun Goddess, which was lost because of man's sin and degradation. The time will come when the human world will end and the new "kingdom of the gods" will arrive for the children of the gods. Until then, the gods are planning to reconstruct human society through the revelations of the founders. The sects teach the coming of the "kingdom of the gods" and try to attain oneness with the will of the Sun Goddess with sincere piety.

Being religions which depend upon revelations, they do not use any scriptures. The gods reveal themselves through the oracles to the founders. The sects do not perform divination, sorcery, or incantation, as the founders have the spiritual insight to foretell future events through the guidance of the gods. They believe in good spirits which are serving and assisting the gods. The sects perform ritual practices for guiding and directing these spirits.

Group Subject to Chinese Influences

There are two sects in the group subject to Chinese influence: Dai Nippon Daido-kyo and Kodo Jingi Inyodo. These teach that the "heavenly way" is the source of all existence, both in the revealed and unrevealed world. The "way" has been one and the same since the beginning of human history and is common to all the races on earth. Man should live in accordance with this will and promote love for fellowmen on the basis of the five principles: (1) benevolence, (2) righteousness, (3) courtesy, (4) knowledge, and (5) trust.

These sects employ prayer, divination, sorcery, incantation, and faith healing transmitted from the ancestors of the founders of the sects. They show strong influences from China, especially dualism, Confucianism, and Taoism.

11

IMPACT OF OCCUPATION ON JAPANESE RELIGIONS

In pre-surrender discussions of the postwar world, no principle, save the basic principle of democracy itself, was more frequently cited than that of religious freedom as essential to the establishment of a permanently peaceful world. While Japanese history has been remarkably free of religious intolerance (presumably because of the part played by Buddhism, the most conspicuously tolerant of the world's religions), the Japanese people have never enjoyed real religious freedom. Throughout the history of the country, one religion or another has enjoyed official protection or patronage to the detriment of non-favored religious groups. During the Tokugawa period, when Christianity was proscribed by the government for political reasons, profession of Buddhism was required of all Japanese as proof that none was Christian. At the beginning of the Meiji period, Buddhism lost its favored position to Shinto. From 1868 to 1945 the principle of unity of government and religion (*saisei ichi*) was zealously followed.

Shrine Shinto, the indigenous Japanese religion which was perverted by militarists to foster a military spirit among the people and to justify wars of expansion, was manufactured into a cult or civic institution termed "State Shinto" or "National Shinto." Acceptance of the official Shinto was made a test of loyalty to the state. Other religions could exist free of molestation only to the extent that they were willing to accommodate themselves to the government's views on Shinto, though a pretence of religious liberty was maintained through the assertion that Shrine Shinto was not to be considered a religion. As such, it was taught in the schools and generally sponsored, supported, perpetuated, and controlled by the state. Every medium known to modern propaganda was used in an attempt to condition all Japanese to unquestioning acceptance of the official views as to the proper nature of society and of political and social morality. The intended effect was to surround the doctrines of militarism and political absolutism with the final sanction of religious belief. Regardless of what other religion a Japanese might profess, he was committed to believe in the official State Shinto story of a land divinely created, of a family of emperors descended in unbroken line from the Sun Goddess, and of a nation of people descended from gods collateral with the ancestors of the imperial family. To express disbelief was to invite prosecution for "dangerous thought."

The Shinto Directive, issued by the Occupation on December 15, 1945, endeavored to separate religion and state by providing for the disestablishment of State Shinto. Equally important, however, was its recognition of Shinto as a religion and its proclamation of equal treatment for all religious groups.

The announced purpose of the Shinto directive was "to separate religion from the state, to prevent misuse of religion for political ends, and to put all religions, faiths, and creeds upon exactly the same basis, entitled to precisely the same opportunities and protection." While virtually prohibiting National (Kokutai) Shinto, it gave Shrine Shinto the same protection extended any other religion. It permitted private support of all Shinto shrines previously supported in whole or in part by public funds, but it required that such private support be entirely voluntary and in no way derived from forced or involuntary contributions.

The directive also called for the annulment of the religious functions order relating to the Grand Shrine of Ise and the religious functions orders relating to state and other shrines, for the abolition of the Shrine Board in the Ministry of Home Affairs, and for the abolition of all public educational institutions whose primary function was either the investigation and dissemination of Shinto or the training of a Shinto priesthood and directed the diversion of their properties to other uses. Under this provision, the Shinto university (Jingu Kogakukan) connected with the Ise Grand Shrine was dissolved. Private educational institutions for the investigation and dissemination of Shinto and for the training of a Shinto priesthood were specifically permitted by the Directive, provided they received no support from public funds.

Elaborating upon the general prohibition and elimination of Shinto from the public schools, the Shinto Directive called for the censorship of all teachers' manuals and textbooks then in use and for the deletion of all Shinto doctrine, prohibited the publication in the future of teachers' manuals and textbooks containing Shinto doctrine, prohibited teaching of Shinto doctrine, prohibited school-sponsored visits to Shinto shrines, called for the immediate removal of all god-shelves, or *kamidana,* and other physical symbols of Shinto, and prohibited discrimination against any teacher or student because of failure to profess and believe in or participate in any practice, rite, ceremony, or observance of Shrine Shinto or of any other religion.

The whole history of Shinto has been intimately connected with members of the imperial family, real and mythological. Amaterasu Shinto was probably created to bolster the position of the heads of the Yamato clan in its struggle with other clans

168

for primacy. In the years before and during the war, Japanese political philosophy became so closely involved with the Shinto cult that it could hardly be understood apart from its interconnection with Shinto. Deliberate and persistent efforts were exerted to make belief in the mythology of the emperor's descent from the Sun Goddess a test of good citizenship. The schools and every means of propaganda were used to instill in Japanese an intense veneration for their emperor. As a direct lineal descendant of the Sun Goddess, the emperor was to many Japanese an actual living god. As such, he was deemed entitled by divine right to rule all lands and all peoples.

The Shinto Directive condemned as ultranationalistic the "doctrine that the emperor of Japan is superior to the heads of other states because of ancestry, descent, or special origin." On January 1, 1946, the emperor issued a rescript labeling as "false" the "conception that the emperor is divine and that Japanese people are superior to other races and fated to rule the world." The Imperial Household Ministry announced that the imperial portraits would no longer be kept in the sacred repositories in schools, but that they would be treated with only that deference normally due to the portraits of the head of a state. The Education Ministry issued a notification calling for the removal of repositories for the imperial portraits from school grounds and, where practical, from school buildings. The Education Ministry also banned ceremonial reading in the public schools of the Imperial Rescript on Education of 1890 and prohibited the school-conducted ceremonies of bowing in the direction of the imperial palace, of shouting "Tenno Heika Banzai" (Long Live the Son of Heaven), and of making other expressions of reverence for the emperor. The Communications and Finance Ministries decided to remove the imperial chrysanthemum crest from future issues of postage stamps and currency, and the Supreme Court ordered the removal of the crest from court buildings.

No restrictions were placed upon the private religious life of the emperor and members of the imperial family. The emperor could conduct services at the shrines located on the palace grounds. As a private individual, he could visit Shinto shrines and send gifts to shrines and other religious institutions. Only in his official capacity as a symbol of the state was the emperor's participation in Shinto rites, ceremonies, and observances prohibited.

The position of the emperor in postwar Japan, thus, involved a compromise which was not always clear-cut in its application. As a private individual, the emperor could practice Shinto beliefs; as the symbol of the state, he had to carefully avoid participation in religious activities. Needless to say, in many specific instances the distinction between the emperor's public and private capacities was difficult to define.

It was a common assertion by many Japanese that religious freedom was established and guaranteed by Article XXVIII of the Meiji Constitution, but a glance at its contents will show why it afforded no real protection. It reads: "Japanese subjects shall, within limits not prejudicial to peace and order, and not antagonistic to their duties as subjects, enjoy freedom of religious belief."

The keystone in the arch of the new religious liberty is the provision in Article 20 of the new Japanese constitution which states that: "Freedom of religion is guaranteed to all. No religious organization shall receive any privileges from the State, nor exercise any political authority. No person shall be compelled to take part in any religious act, celebration, rite or practice." This succinct and unequivocal guarantee is in marked contrast with the watered-down provision of the Meiji Constitution. The new constitution was definite and specific in its prohibition of religious instruction in the public schools. Article 20 provided that "the State and its organs shall refrain from religious education or any religious activity."

Perhaps the most publicized result of the removal of restrictions on religious liberty has been the numerous withdrawals of temples, churches, and sub-sects from parent sects. For several centuries Tokugawa hostility to any change in the social order and the predilection of post-Meiji Restoration governments for dealing only with large groups prevented any break-up in established religious orders and made extremely difficult the rise of new sects. The new Religious Bodies Law of 1939 forced further merging of religious sects and denominations. It is not strange, then, that when age-old restrictions were removed withdrawals from old sects should immediately begin. These withdrawals appear to have been due in part to a desire to escape from compulsory wartime unions, in part to a feeling that parent sects had been oppressive and parasitical, in part to genuine differences in matters of religious substance, and in part to a feeling that independence was in keeping with the spirit of the times.

Today, the separation of religion and state in Japan is as complete as in any country in the world. State Shinto has been disestablished as a compulsory national faith; the burden of compulsory financial support of State Shinto has been lifted from the Japanese people; Shinto doctrines and observances have been removed from the public educational system and Shrine Shinto has been recognized as a religion, enjoying the same status as the other religions in Japan. The constitution guarantees separation of religion and state as clearly and unequivocally as any of the other written constitutions of the world.

STATISTICS OF RELIGIOUS SECTS AND DENOMINATIONS[a]

(Source: Reports Submitted by Sect Headquarters in 1946[b])

Sects	Installations	Workers	Adherents
I. BUDDHISM			
A. Amida School			
1. Ji	414	559	332,100
2. Jodo Sects			
a. Jodo[c]	(9,172)[c]	(18,631)[c]	(4,520,535)[c]
(1) Jodo	—	—	—
(2) Kurodani Jodo	52	—	350,000
b. Jodo Seizan[d]	(1,474)[d]	(2,339)[d]	(609,679)[d]
(1) Jodo Seizan	—	—	—
(2) Fudan Nembutsu	10	69	22,600
3. Jodo Shin Sects			
a. Bukkoji[e]	(384)[e]	(818)[e]	(172,167)[e]
(1) Bukkoji	—	—	—
(2) Jokoji	10	10	10,436
b. Izumoji	79	160	34,220
c. Joshoji	53	138	89,292
d. Koshoji	563	1,107	135,217

a Caution should be exercised in using religious statistics for comparative purposes inasmuch as they are based on varying standards of computation.
b Unless otherwise indicated.
c Figures in parentheses represent totals claimed by Jodo Sect before secession of Kurodani Jodo.
d Figures in parentheses represent totals claimed by Jodo Seizan Sect before secession of Fudan Nembutsu.
e Figures in parentheses represent totals claimed by Bukkoji Sect before secession of Jokoji.

Sects	Installations	Workers	Adherents
e. Kibe	208	750	100,215
f. Nishi-Honganji	10,761	33,118	7,378,571
g. Otani	9,582	29,503	8,484,200
h. Sammonto	62	113	8,434
i. Takada	692	1,013	95,020
j. Yamamoto	21	83	1,200
4. Shinshu	—	—	—
5. Yuzu Nembutsu	372	346	99,150
B. Nara School			
1. Hosso	77	954	57,042
2. Kegon	125	523	50,915
3. Ritsu	45	96	27,897
C. Nichiren School			
1. Hokke	751	1,500	459,987
2. Hommon Butsuryu[f]	(166)[f]	(415)[f]	(308,549)[f]
a. Hommon Butsuryu	—	—	—
b. Nichiren Shugi Butsuryuko	—	—	—
3. Myo Hokke	17	37	30,129
4. Nakayama Myo	10	43	102,000
5. Nichiren[g]	(5,421)[g]	(6,111)[g]	(897,984)[g]
a. Nichiren	—	—	—
b. Honge Myo	—	2	175
c. Shinto-en	—	1	90
6. Nichiren Komon	7	12	4,500
7. Nichiren Sho	135	329	128,520
8. Showa Hon	—	—	50
9. Zaike Nichiren Jofukai	—	—	—
D. Shingon School			
1. Birushana	2	—	530
2. Busan	3,075	4,671	1,371,820
3. Chisan	3,257	5,260	1,101,000

f Figures is parentheses represent totals claimed by Hommon Butsuryu Sect before secession of Nichiren Shugi Butsuryuko.

g Figures in parentheses represent totals claimed by Nichiren Sect before secessions by Honge Myo and Shinto-en.

Sects	Installations	Workers	Adherents
4. Daigo	1,372	6,767	816,766
5. Kokubunji	—	—	—
6. Koyasan Shingon[h]	(3,762)[h]	(11,322)[h]	(4,221,110)[h]
a. Koyasan Shingon	—	—	—
b. Gochi Kyodan	5	—	1,000
c. Kannonshu	1	—	200,000
d. Reiunji	31	38	35,950
e. Shugen	109	—	23,808
f. Sumadera	4	—	1,400
7. Nakayama Shingo Sho	60	—	350,000
8. Omuro	1,285	945	900,750
9. Sennyuji	44	108	14,027
10. Shin Bukkyo Kukai	—	—	—
11. Shingon Ritsu	71	113	67,858
12. Shin Shingon	—	—	2,500
13. Shoden	5	5	400
14. Toji	209	589	39,600
15. Yamashina	172	763	35,000
16. Zentsuji	74	457	32,144
E. Tendai School			
1. Jimon	746	1,809	79,290
2. Shinsei	438	344	27,618
3. Shugen	195	1,464	29,200
4. Tendai	(3,708)	(6,880)	(1,137,671)
a. Tendai	—	—	—
b. Haguroyama Shugen Honshu	4	4	—
c. Shugendo	—	—	—
F. Zen School			
1. Obaku[j]	(516)[j]	(837)[j]	(118,224)[j]
a. Obaku	—	—	—
b. Guze	1	—	5,000

h Figures in parentheses represent totals claimed by Koyasan Shingon Sect before secessions by Gochi Kyodan, Kannonshu, Reiunji, Shugen, and Sumadera.
j Figures in parentheses represent totals claimed by Obaku Sect before secession of Guze.

Sects	Installations	Workers	Adherents
2. Rinzai			
a. Buttsuji	51	83	53,100
b. Daitokuji	206	332	91,784
c. Eigenji	137	183	45,740
d. Enkakuji	210	280	86,050
e. Hakoji	178	259	13,840
f. Kenchoji	420	562	165,414
g. Kenninji	74	104	16,865
h. Kagakuji	38	30	18,050
i. Kokutaiji	34	53	21,067
j. Myoshinji	3,610	7,109	1,316,759
k. Nanzenji	424	727	266,223
l. Ryobo-zen	—	—	2,479
m. Shokokuji	112	181	138,640
n. Tenryuji	116	173	44,838
o. Tofukuji	397	671	50,000
3. Shobo	—	—	—
4. Soto	14,895	31,084	6,408,622
G. Unclassified Sects			
1. Anna Kyodan	4	—	—
2. Bukkyo Seidokyodan	59	—	50,000
3. Daimoku	—	—	—
4. Isson	4	8	631
5. Koankai	13	—	1,232
6. Myoken	—	—	—
7. Nyorai	73	146	63,530
8. Shinri Undo	1	9	10,000
II. CHRISTIANITY[k]			
A. Catholic[l]	(332)[l]	(404)[l]	(108,324)[l]
B. Christian Brotherhood	26	61	1,200
C. Church of Christ[m]	(1,800)[m]	(2,800)[m]	(200,000)[m]
D. Episcopal[m]	(215)[m]	(249)[m]	(19,036)[m]
E. Immanuel Church	13	26	549

k Christian statistics purport to claim actual church members only.
l Katoriku Shimbun (Catholic Newspaper), 15 January 1947.
m Reports from Headquarters during July 1947.

Sects	Installations	Workers	Adherents
F. International Christian Church	8	—	445
G. Jesus Society[m]	(12)[m]	(28)[m]	(1,000)[m]
H. Living Water Church	13	30	1,129
I. Oriental Missionary Society[m]	(7)[m]	(13)[m]	(400)[m]
J. Orthodox	167	42	13,990
K. Reformed Church	9	9	215
L. Salvation Army[m]	(48)[m]	(184)[m]	(5,000)[m]
M. Seventh Day Adventist[m]	(24)[m]	(56)[m]	(800)[m]
N. Yokohama Fukuin Iryo Sendyodan	7	4	100
III. SECTARIAN SHINTO			
A. Fuso[n]	(463)[n]	(3,049)[n]	(384,753)[n]
1. Fuso	—	—	—
2. Ishizuchi	48	—	100,000
3. Jitsugetsu	22	86	14,980
4. Kiso Mitake	5	—	580
5. Makotono Michi	1	59	5,134
6. P. L. Kyodan	14	—	3,000
7. Shinsei	—	—	—
8. Shinto Teruo	—	—	—
9. Seisei	15	—	2,380
10. Shiogama	2	—	380
11. Sogo Gimin	1	—	1,100
12. Tenchi	2	—	1,500
B. Jikko[o]	(612)[o]	(2,643)[o]	(221,038)[o]
1. Jikko	—	—	—
2. Meiji	42	130	61,600
3. Myosho	—	8	168
4. Shinto Kompira	—	—	—

n Figures in parentheses represent totals claimed by Fuso Sect before secession of Ishizuchi, Jitsugetsu, Kiso Mitake, Makotono Michi, P. L. Kyodan, Shinsei, Shinto Teruo, Seisei, Shiogama, Sogo Gimin, and Tenchi.

o Figures in parentheses represent totals claimed by Jikko Sect before secession of Meiji, Myosho, and Shinto Kompira.

Sects	Installations	Workers	Adherents
C. Konko	1,540	2,637	683,036
D. Kurozumi	433	3,409	574,032
E. Misogi	46	777	83,401
F. Mitake[p]	(861)[p]	(9,533)[p]	(1,647,573)[p]
1. Mitake	—	—	—
2. Hino	2	—	3,000
3. Hinomoto	—	—	13,345
4. Naobi	7	14	1,556
5. Ontakekyo Shusei	3	7	819
6. Shinreikai	278	—	101,563
G. Shinri[q]	(397)[q]	(4,187)[q]	(346,143)[q]
1. Shinri	—	—	—
2. Seiko	118	—	256,140
3. Meisei	—	—	—
4. Uchu	—	—	—
H. Shinshu[r]	(233)[r]	(2,923)[r]	(401,000)[r]
1. Shinshu	—	—	—
2. Meisei	11	—	—
3. Dainichi	—	—	6,800
4. Nikko	12	246	12,539
5. Shinso	16	—	9,077
I. Shusei	385	1,676	43,584
J. Tai (Shinto Honkyoku)[s]	(997)[s]	(5,289)[s]	(1,091,078)[s]
1. Tai	—	—	—
2. Bosei	6	—	5,380
3. Hinomoto	2	—	—
4. Maruyama	46	—	102,530
5. Shinto Ishikiri	8	150	71,000
6. Shinto Kotodama	—	—	10

p Figures in parentheses represent totals claimed by Mitake Sect before secessions by Hino, Hinomoto, Naobi, Ontakekyo, Shusei, and Shinreikai.

q Figures in parentheses represent totals claimed by Shinri Sect before secessions by Seiko, Meisei, and Uchu.

r Figures in parentheses represent totals claimed by Shinshu Sect before secessions by Meisei, Dainichi, Nikko, and Shinso.

s Figures in parentheses represent totals claimed by Tai Sect before secessions by Bosei, Hinomoto, Maruyama, Shinto Ishikiri, Shinto Kotodama, Shinto Kotoku, Shinto Seitai, and Tengyokyo.

Sects	Installations	Workers	Adherents
7. Shinto Kotoku	4	61	45,000
8. Shinto Seitai	—	—	—
9. Tengyokyo	44	124	1,420
K. Taisei[t]	(199)[t]	(1,404)[t]	(135,000)[t]
1. Taisei	—	—	—
2. Shugendo	50	581	27,360
3. Daido	—	—	—
L. Taisha	367	20,146	3,404,983
M. Tenri[u]	(11,978)[u]	(76,315)[u]	(1,158,414)[u]
1. Tenri	—	—	—
2. Taido	—	—	—
3. Tenri Hommichi	—	—	—
4. Yuishin Remmei	—	—	—

IV. SHRINE SHINTO[v]

	Installations	Workers	Adherents
A. Hakuzan	1	14	100,000
B. Hokkaido Minami Jinja	77	25	60,000
C. Inari	47	—	5,000
D. Jinja Honcho	86,197	15,393	—
E. Jinja Honkyo	132	—	—
F. Jinja Ubusuna	14	—	—
G. Kiso Mitake Honkyo	6	—	880
H. Shimmei Kyodan	—	—	500
I. Shinto Dairei	20	—	1,800
J. Soshin-no Miyashiro Honkyo	1	—	2,400
K. Tenshokyo Hombu	—	—	—

V. UNCLASSIFIED SECTS

	Installations	Workers	Adherents
A. Ainu	—	—	—
B. Aizen-en	185	148	13,000
C. Dai Nippon Daidokyo	13	45	15,415
D. Daisokyo	—	—	150

[t] Figures in parentheses represent totals claimed by Taisei Sect before secessions of Shugendo and Daido.

[u] Figures in parentheses represent totals claimed by Tenri Sect before secessions of Taido, Tenri Hommichi, and Yuishin Remmei.

[v] Jinja Honcho (Shrine Association) reported that, as of 1 March 1947, 18,920 shrines had been dissolved, and that 88,463 shrines remained.

RELIGIONS IN JAPAN

Sects	Installations	Workers	Adherents
E. Dokai	1	—	10,000
F. Hinomoto Kyodan	4	—	11,000
G. Jiukyo	—	—	—
H. Kodo Chikyo Onnyodo	3	3	6,300
I. Minseikyo	1	1	30
J. Mohammedan	4		490
K. Nichiren Kyosha	5	—	1,346
L. Nichizen-kyo	24	3	10,000
M. Nikko Honkyo	—	—	—
N. Renshindo	25	35	2,400
O. Seicho-no-Ie	2,004	—	1,000,000
P. Seisei Kyodan	1	7	860
Q. Shidaido Shindo	—	—	—
R. Shimboku Kyodan	39	300	35,800
S. Shimmei-kyo	—	—	—
T. Shinri-kyo	1	—	1,380
U. Sugawara Kyodan	—	—	—
V. Sumera-kyo	21	—	117,199
W. Tenrei-kyo	—	—	10,000
X. Tensho Kotai Jingukyo	17	17	21,200
Y. Yamato-kyo	23		5,300

GLOSSARY OF RELIGIOUS TERMS

ama	Buddhist nun
amadera	Buddhist nunnery
anshurei	Christian ordination
bansan-shiki	communion service
betsuin	branch temple
bochi	graveyard
bodaiji	family temple
bokushi	Christian pastor
Bukkyo	Buddhism
Butsuda	Buddha
butsudan	Buddhist family god-shelf
butsuji	Buddhist service
chigi	wooden cross-pieces standing at extremities of ridge pole of shrine
chinju	Shinto tutelary deity
daishikyo	Christian archibishop
daisojo	Buddhist patriarch
danka	Buddhist parishioner
dannadera	family temple
doshi	officiator at Buddhist service
gasshotai	choir
gofu	Shinto talisman
gohei	Shinto symbol of divinity made of cut paper
gojo	the five great virtues of Confucianism
goju-no-to	pagoda
Gokuraku	Sukhavati, or Buddhist Paradise
gonguji	Vice-chief priest of a shrine
gorin	the five great Confucian ethical relationships

guji	chief priest of a shrine
haiden	outer worship hall of shrine
haka	grave
hakaba	graveyard
harai	exorcism
harisutosu-sei-kyo-kai	Greek Orthodox Church
hojo	chief priest of temple
honden	sanctuary of shrine
hondo	main temple in compound
honji	head temple
honsha	head shrine
honzan	head temple
honzon	principal image in temple
Hotoke	Buddha
Ikibotoke	Living Buddha
inori	Christian prayer
Jigoku	Naraka, or Buddhist Hell
jiin	temple
jingu	state-supported shrine
jinja	shrine
Jinja Shinto	Shrine Shinto
jujika	cross
junrei	Buddhist pilgrim
jushoku	chief priest of temple
juzu	Buddhist beads
kagura	sacred Shinto dance
kagura-den	pavilion in shrine for sacred dance
kamidana	Shinto family god-shelf
kane	bell of temple
kanetsukido	bell tower of temple
kannushi	Shinto priest
kantoku	Christian bishop
kashiwade	hand-clapping before Shinto sanctuary
katsuo-gi	cigar-shaped decorations on ridge pole of shrine
kenkin	offering (Christian)
keshin	incarnation
kesa	Buddhist priest's stole
Kirisutan	Christian
Kirisuto	Christ
kito	Christian prayer

kitokai	Christian prayer meeting
kodan	pulpit
kige	incense and flowers for Buddhist service
Kokka Shinto	State Shinto
koromo	Buddhist priest's robe
kozo	Buddhist disciple
kudoku	Buddhist merit
kuri	Buddhist priest's living quarters
kyo	sutra or scripture
kyoekisha	Christian priest
Kyoha Shinto	Sectarian Shinto
kyokai	Christian church
kyomon	Buddhist sutra
Kyoseigun	Salvation Army
massha	branch shrine
matsuji	branch temple
matsuri	Shinto festival
mikagami	sacred mirror in shrine
miko	maiden in service of a shrine
mikoshi	sacred portable shrine
mikuji	divination
misogi	Shinto purification
mitama	spirit or soul (Shinto)
mitama-shiro	Shinto substitute-spirit or symbol of divinity
mitarashi	Shinto ablution basin
miya	shrine
mon	shrine crest or symbol
mukakusha	lesser shrine without rank
negi	Shinto priest of inferior rank
nichiyo gakko	Sunday school
Niomon	two-king gates of temple
niso	Buddhist priestess
norito	Shinto written prayer
nusa	Shinto symbol of divinity made of twisted rope
ofuda	Shinto talisman
onna-shitsuji	Christian deaconess
o-shimeshi	divine guidance
osho	chief priest of temple
reihai	Christian worship or adoration
reikon	spirit or soul (Christian)

Ryobu Shinto	dual-aspect Shinto
saibun	ceremonial message to Shinto deity
saiden	altar
saisei-ichi	the unity of rites and government
saisen	offering of money
saisen-bako	offertory box
saishi	religious ceremonies
sakaki	*Eurya Ocunacea*; sacred tree of Shinto
sambika	hymn
Sammi-ittai	Trinity
sammon	main gate of temple
seijin	Christian saint
sesan-shiki	communion service
seisho	bible
senkyoshi	missionary
senreiban	font
senrei-shiki	baptism
shamusho	shrine office
shihen	psalm
shikimi	sacred branch placed on Buddhist grave
shimboku	sacred tree in shrine compound
shimenawa	sacred Shinto festoon made of rope
shinden	sanctuary of shrine
shingakko	Christian theological seminary
shinja	layman (Christian or Buddhist)
shinjo	creed
shinkan	Shinto priest
Shinkyo-Kyokai	Protestant Church
shinshoku	Shinto priest
shintai	Shinto symbol of divinity; god-body
Shinto	Shinto, or the Way of the Gods
shito	Christian apostle
shitsuji	Christian deacon
shonin	Buddhist saint
shoro	bell tower of temple
shu	sect (Buddhism)
shudoin	monastery
shudojo	Christian nun
Shuha Shinto	Sectarian Shinto
shukke	Buddhist priest
shukuto	benediction
soin	temple
soryo	Buddhist priest
sotoba	stupa

sukeisha	devotees of a particular shrine
taishi	Buddhist saint or celebrated teacher
tamagushi	Shinto offering of a sakaki branch
tamashii	spirit or soul (Christian)
Tenshuko-Kyokai	Catholic Church
tera	temple
tera-otoko	man in service of a temple
to	steeple
torii	shrine gateway
tsurigane	bell of temple
ujigami	Shinto tutelary deity
ujiko	Shinto parishioner
yashiro	shrine

BIBLIOGRAPHY

General Works

Anesaki, Masaharu, *Religious Life of the Japanese People*, (reprint from vol. II of "Series on Japanese Life and Culture"), (Tokyo, Society for International Cultural Relations, 1938).
> Probably the best brief treatment of the religious systems of Japan.

Anesaki, Masaharu, *History of Japanese Religion*, (London, Kegan Paul, 1930).
> An excellent history of Japanese religions with special reference to their contributions to the social and moral life of the nation.

Brumbauch, T. T., *Religious Values in Japanese Culture*, (Tokyo, Christian Literature Society, 1934).
> A summary treatment of the religious elements of the various religious systems in Japan, written with a slight Christian bias.

Griffis, William E., *The Religions of Japan*, (New York, Scribner's, 1895).
> An old but still useful history of Japanese religions which carries through the Tokugawa period.

Harada, Tasuku, *The Faith of Japan*, (New York, Macmillan, 1914).
> An attempt to treat Japanese religious life as a union of elements from all religions which have affected the thought and life of the people.

Shinto

Aston, W. G., *Shinto, the Way of the Gods*, (London, Longman, 1905).
> A scholarly treatment of the development of Shinto, dealing mainly with the Old Shinto of the classical age.

187

BIBLIOGRAPHY

Ballou, Robert O., *Shinto, the Unconquered Enemy*, (New York, Viking Press, 1945).
    A brief survey of the development and nature of the doctrine of racial superiority and world conquest which characterized State Shinto, particularly valuable for its quotations from Japanese Texts. Follows Holtom.

Holtom, D. C., *Modern Japan and Shinto Nationalism*, (Chicago, University of Chicago Press, 1943).
    An attempt to explain how Shinto was used by Japanese militarists and ultranationalists and to describe the impact of this effort on Buddhism and Christianity.

Holtom, D. C., *The National Faith of Japan*, (London, Kegan Paul, 1937).
    The standard authority in English on Shinto, dealing comprehensively with both State Shinto and Sect Shinto.

Holtom, D. C., *The Political Philosophy of Modern Shinto*, (in Transactions of the Asiatic Society of Japan, Vol. 49, no. 2, 1922).
    A comprehensive study of the politico-religious situation in Japan.

Kato, Genchi, *A Study of Shinto, the Religion of the Japanese Nation*, (Tokyo, Meiji Japan Society, 1926).
    A sympathetic treatment of Shinto by the best-known contemporary Japanese Shinto scholar.

Mason, J. W. T., *The Meaning of Shinto*, (New York, Dutton, 1935).
    A general non-critical treatment of Shinto by one of the few Occidentals who has embraced the Shinto faith.

Buddhism

Armstrong, R. C., *Buddhism and Buddhists in Japan*, (London, Macmillan, 1927).
    A concise survey of Japanese Buddhism.

Eliot, Sir Charles, *Japanese Buddhism*, (London, Arnold, 1935).
    Probably the most authoritative work in English on Japanese Buddhism, though some Japanese scholars have criticized it as not giving proper recognition to the special characteristics of Japanese Buddhism.

Lloyd, Arthur, *The Creed of Half Japan*, (London, Murray, 1911).
    A pioneer work in English embracing the development and doctrines of Japanese Buddhism.

Pratt, J. B., *The Pilgrimage of Buddhism and a Buddhist Pilgrim*, (New York, Macmillan, 1928).

> A survey of the movement of Buddhism from India to Japan with an attempt to describe Buddhism as it is actually lived in the various countries of Asia today.

Reischauer, A. K., *Studies in Japanese Buddhism*, (New York, Macmillan, 1917).

> A valuable survey of the development and doctrine of Japanese Buddhism.

Herold, A. Ferdinand, *The Life of Buddha*, translated from the French by Paul Blum, (Tokyo, Tuttle, 1954).

> A factual biography of the historical Buddha based on Indian legends, poems, history, and literature.

Christianity

Japan Christian Year Book, (Tokyo, Christian Literature Society, 1903–1941).

> A detailed yearly account of the Protestant Christian Movement in Japan, usually including brief chapters on Catholicism.

Laures, Johannes, *Kirishitan Bunko. A Manual of Books and Documents on the Early Christian Missions in Japan*, (Tokyo, Sophia University, 1940, with supplements, 1941 and 1951).

> A detailed and extremely complete bibliography covering material from the first letters through the period of restoration of the Japanese mission 1865–1880).

Laures, Johannes, *The Catholic Church in Japan, A Short History*, (Tokyo, Tuttle, 1954).

> A scholarly yet highly readable account of the progress of the Catholic Church in Japan from its earliest beginings through its latest developments.

Laymen's Foreign Missions Inquiry, Re-thinking Missions, Supplementary Series, vols. 3–4, Japan, (New York, Harper, 1933).

> A comprehensive and critical inquiry into the organization, activities, and aims of the Protestant Christian Movement in Japan.

INDEX

"Age of the gods," 7
Amaterasu Omikami. *See* Sun Goddess
Ame-no-minakanushi, 103, 140
Amida. *See* Buddha Amida; *also* Buddhism, Amida school of
Ancestor worship, primitive form of, 2; Chinese influence on, 11, 115
Anti-Buddhist feeling, 28
Ashikaga Period, 17–19
Astrology, Shinto priests' adoption of, 104

Black magic, 113–14
Bodhidharma, 88, 89
Bodhisattva Daiseishi, 78, 82
Bodhisattva Kwannon, 78, 82
Bodhisattvas, 48
Bosatsu Jogyo, 93, 95
Buddha Amida, 48, 74–85
Buddha Dainichi, 48, 69
Buddha Hall, 54
Buddha S'akyamuni. *See* S'akyamuni Gautama
Buddhism, Amida school of, 74–87; during Ashikaga Period, 17–19; description of sects, 58–97; outline history of, 4–26; introduction to Japan, 4–8; during Heian Period, 8–12; institutional aspects of, 49–57; Ji Sect of, 82–83; Jimon Sect of, 66–67; Jodo & Jodo Seizan Sects of, 80–82; Jodo Shin Sect of, 83–87; during Kamakura Period, 12–17; since Meiji Restoration, 25–26; Nara Sects of, 59–61; Nichiren school of, 92–97; priesthood of, 51–53; Obaku Sect of, 92; Rinzai school of, 91; scriptures, sacred utensils & services, 55–57; Shingon school of, 69–74; Shinsei Sect

of, 68; Shugen Sect of, 67–68; Soto Sect of 91–92; sect organization of, 49–50; temples of, 53–55; Tendai school of, 61–68; Tendai Sect of, 65–66; during Tokugawa Period, 23–25; Yuzu Nembutsu Sect of, 79–80; Zen school of, 87–92
Buppo, 6
Bushido, 90
Butsudan, 5

Census register, use of Buddhist registration as, 23
Chinese dualism, influence on divination and fortunetelling, 106; theory of five elements in, 105; and new sects, 161, 165; influence on Shinto, 104–06; *yin* and *yang* principles of, 105
Christianity, educational programs of, 157–59; control by government of, 33–37; early history of, 148–50; recent history of, 151–55; introduction to Japan of, 20–22; welfare work of, 155–57
Confucianism, influence on ancestor worship, 11, 106; early contact with Buddhism, 45; influence on Buddhist morality, 47–48; relationship to *bushido*, 90; practical ethics of, 5; introduction of, 3; and Loyalist Movement, 106; Mito school of, 24, 106; and new sects, 161, 165; and Sectarian Shinto, 130, 131, 135–36; influence on Shinto, 106; Shusei and Taisei Sects of, 135–36; Shushi school of, 90, 106; influence on Tokugawa feudalism, 23–24, 106; relationship to Zen, 23, 90

191

"Cosmic Buddha." *See* Buddha Dainichi

Daikokuten, 112
Dengyo Daishi (Saicho), 9–10, 62
Divination, in primitive religion, 2; by Shinto shrines, 11, 123; in Sectarian Shinto, 136, 138, 139, 140; in new sects, 161, 163
"Divine wind," 42
Dogen, 88; *See also*, Buddhism, Soto Sect of
Dokyo, 8
Doso-jin, 112
Dual-aspect Shinto. *See* Ryobu Shinto
"Dust," 145
Dutch in Japan, 22, 149

Education, religious sponsorship of, 135, 146, 157–59
Eisai, 15, 88; *See also*, Buddhism, Rinzai Sect of
Emperor worship, 108, 109, 116; *See also*, Tennoism in
Enchin, 66
Ennin, 66
En-no-Shokaku, 67
Enryakuji, 62, 65
Esoteric practices. *See* Mysticism
Exorcism, by Shinto shrines, 11; in Sectarian Shinto, 138, 139, 140

Faith healing, in Sectarian Shinto, 131, 138, 141, 143, 147; in new sects, 165
Fortunetelling, 136
Fuji, Mount, in Mountain Sects, 137, 138
Fujiwara family, 8, 9, 60

Genshin, 68
Geomancy, Shinto priests' adoption of, 104
God-body, 126
God-shelf, 110–11
Gohei, 121
Gokoku shrines, 41, 127–28
Government, role of in religious life, 27–43
"Great father of the universe," of Konko-kyo, 143–44
Great Parent God, of Tenri-kyo, 131

Hachiman shrines, 124–25
Haiden, 119
Hasegawa, founder of Fuji worship, 137
"Heavenly reason," 29
Heian Period, 8–12
Henotheism. *See* Sun worship
Hideyoshi, 20, 149
Hiei, Mount, 62, 65
Hojo family, 13
Honden, 119
Honen, 14, 17, 75, 80; *See also*, Buddhism, Jodo & Jodo Seizan Sects of
Honganji, 86
Horyuji, 60

Iemitsu, 22
Ieyasu, 20, 22, 149–50
Imperial Rescript on Education, 31, 109, 169
Inari shrines, 125
Ingen, 92
Ippen, 82–83; *See also*, Buddhism, Ji Sect of
Ise Grand Shrine, 6, 110, 122, 123, 126
Izanagi and Izanami, 3, 103

Jimmu Tenno, 3, 104

Kagawa, Toyohiko, 153
Kakuban, 72
Kamado-no-kami, 112
Kamakura Period, 12–17
Kami 2, 99–100
Kamidana. See God-shelf
Kamikaze, 42
Kami-musubi, 103
Kashiwara Shrine, 127
Kawade, founder of Konko-kyo, 143
Kennyo, 86
Kobo Daishi (Kukai), 9–10, 69
Kofukuji, 60
Kojiki, 7, 103
Kokutai, 109
Kongobuji, 73
Koya, Mount, 69, 73
Kukai. *See* Kobo Daishi
Kurozumi Munetada, founder of Kuro-zumi-kyo, 142–43
Kwammu, Emperor, 9, 62, 69
Kyonyo, 87

Lamaism, 73
Legends, 1–3, 103–04
Lotus sutra, 15, 16, 62–63, 93, 96

Magic, Shinto priests' adoption of, 104; popular faith in, 114
Mandala, 71
Meiji Period, 23–33, 106–09
Meiji Shrine, 127
Militarism in Religion, 37–42
Mitamashiro, 126
Mito school of Confucianism, 24, 106
Mongol invasion, 17, 94
Myojin, Shinto guardian diety of temples, 66
Myoshinji, 91
Mysticism, of Shingon Buddhism, 69–73
Mythology, 3, 102–04

Nakayama Miki, founder of Tenri-kyo, 145
"National structure," 42, 109
Nature worship, 1, 99, 115, 130
Necromancy, 113–14
Nembutsu, 78, 84
New Sects, 160–65; monotheistic group of, 162; henotheistic group of, 163; Shinto polytheistic group of, 163–64; messianic group of, 164–65; group subject to Chinese influence, 165
Nichiren, 15, 92–95; See also, Buddhism, Nichiren school of
Ninigi-no-mikoto, 3
Nihongi, 7 ,24, 103
Nirvana, 44
Nobunaga, 20, 149

Occupation, impact on Japanese religions, 166–171
Okuni-nushi-no-mikoto, 134
Onjoji, 66, 67
Ontake, Mount, 137, 138
Onyo-do, 106

Pagoda, 54
Pali sutras, 56
Pantheism, 123
"People's ceremony," 39
Perry, Commodore, 25
Phallicism, 101, 112

Portuguese in Japan, 20, 22
Primitive religion, 1–3; polytheism in, 1; animism in, 1, 99; anthropomorphism in, 1, 100; nature worship in, 2, 99; ancestor worship in, 2, 100; phallicism in, 101; purification rites in, 2; absence of speculative elements in, 100; "Pure land," 74; See also, Buddhism, Jodo & Jodo Seizan Sects of; and Buddhism, Jodo Shin Sect of
Purification rites, in new sects, 164; popularity of, 113; in primitive religion, 2; in Sectarian Shinto, 130, 131, 134, 136, 137, 139, 140

Religious Bodies Law, 33–35, 153, 171
Religious League, 34, 43
Rennyo, 84
Ryobu (dual-aspect) Shinto, 10, 70, 105, 116
Ryonin, 74–75, 79–80; See also, Buddhism, Yuzu Nembutsu Sect of

Saicho. See Dengyo Daishi
Sakaki tree, 111, 119
S'akyamuni Gautama, 44–45, 47–48; in Jodo school, 82; in Nichiren school, 93
Seisei ichi, 28, 166
Sengoku Period, 20
Shamanism, 116
Shinran, 15, 17, 76–77, 83–84; See also, Buddhism, Jodo Shin Sect of
Shinsei, 68
Shintai, 126
Shinto, origin of name of, 6; Imperial Family, 110; Household, 110–111; Meiji revival of, 27–32; early mythology of, 102–04; nature and types of, 98–114; popular beliefs of, 112–14; primitive forms of, 99–102, Ryobu, 10; Tennoism, 108–10
Shinto, Sectarian, 129–47; Confucian sects of, 135–36; mountain sects of, 136–39; peasant sects of 141–47; pure Shinto sects of, 132–35; purification sects of, 139–41
Shinto, Shrine, 115–28; buildings of, 119–20; priesthood of, 118–19; types of shrines of, 121–28; worship in, 120–21
Shoku, 82

Shotoku Taishi, 4
"Shrine system," 31, 117
Shushi school of Confucianism, 23, 90, 106
Social welfare, religious sponsorship of, 131, 135, 144, 146, 155–57
Sorcery, in primitive religion, 2; popular faith in, 114; in new sects, 161, 163, 165
Spirit possession, 112, 113
Substitute spirit, 102, 126
Suiko, Empress, 4
Sun Goddess, 3, 6, 28, 101–04, 126–27, 163, 164
Sun worship, 3, 103, 161
Sutra, 45, 56

Taika Reform, 5
Takami-musubi, 103
Takehaya-susanowo, 103
Tantric Buddhism, 73
Taoism, and animism, 105; and ascetic practices, 105; contact with early Buddhism, 45–46; introduction of, 3; and new sects, 165; and Sectarian Shinto, 137; influence on Shinto, 104, 105, 116
Todaiji, 61
Tokugawa Period, 20–25
Torii, 98, 102, 119, 120, 136
Toshodaiji, 61
Tsuki-yomi, 103

Wani, 3
"Way of the gods," 6, 98; in Sectarian Shinto, 133, 138, 139
"Way of humanity," 29
Western Paradise, 14, 74
Witchcraft, 113–14

Xavier, St. Francis, 20, 148–49

Yamato clan, 1–3, 102, 108, 168
Yasukuni Shrine, 41, 126–28
Yasushiji, 60